P9-DCF-078

STECK-VAUGHN

Target SPELLING 360

Margaret Scarborough
Mary F. Brigham
Teresa A. Miller

STECK-VAUGHN
ELEMENTARY · SECONDARY · ADULT · LIBRARY

A Harcourt Company

www.steck-vaughn.com

Table of Contents

Acknowledgments

Editorial Director:	Stephanie Muller
Editor:	Kathleen Gower Wiseman
Associate Director of Design:	Cynthia Ellis
Design Managers:	Sheryl Cota, Katie Nott
Illustrators:	Peg Dougherty, Jimmy Longacre, Cindy Aarvig, David Griffin, Lynn McClain
Cover Design:	Bassett & Brush Design, Todd Disrud and Stephanie Schreiber

ISBN 0-7398-2457-0
Copyright © 2001 Steck-Vaughn Company
All rights reserved. No part of the material protected by this copyright may be reproduced or utilized in any form or by any means, electronic or mechanical, including photocopying, recording, or by any information storage and retrieval system, without permission in writing from the copyright owner. Requests for permission to make copies of any part of the work should be mailed to: Copyright Permissions, Steck-Vaughn Company, P.O. Box 26015, Austin, TX 78755. Printed in the United States of America.

1 2 3 4 5 6 7 8 9 DBH 04 03 02 01 00

Word Study Plan

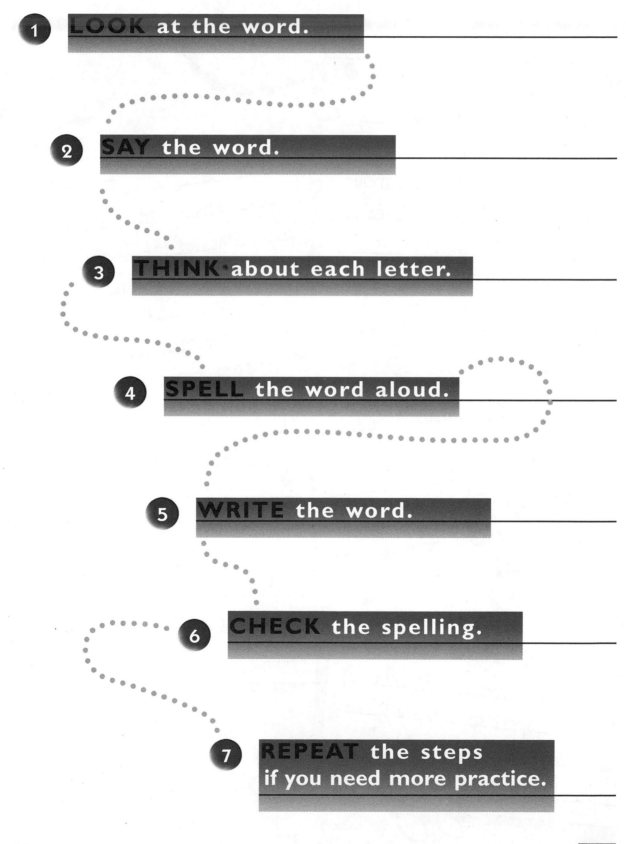

1 **LOOK** at the word. _____

2 **SAY** the word. _____

3 **THINK** about each letter. _____

4 **SPELL** the word aloud. _____

5 **WRITE** the word. _____

6 **CHECK** the spelling. _____

7 **REPEAT** the steps
if you need more practice. _____

© 2001 Steck-Vaughn Company. All Rights Reserved.

Name _____

Spelling Strategies

plant
play
please

cat, bat, hat

Think about the beginning sound of the word that you want to spell. Then think about a word you know that begins with the same sound.

Look for word families. The first letters of the words in a word family are different. The other letters are the same. Words in a word family rhyme.

Think about the shape of each letter in the word.

s h i p

If you are not sure how to spell a word, take a guess. Then look up the word in the dictionary.

Think about how a word is spelled and then write it. Try different spellings. Look at each spelling to see if it looks right.

skatee
skate ✓
skat

doc • tor

Words with *bl-*

bled	black	woman
block	blend	wonder

DAY 1

A **Circle the spelling word. Then write it on the line.**

1. I (wonder) where I left my books. _wonder_

2. He had to blend the paints together. _____

3. The man wore a black coat. _____

4. A girl will grow up to be a woman. _____

5. They live on the same block. _____

6. When I cut my hand, it bled. _____

B **Circle the word that is the same as the top one.**

bled	blend	black	block	wonder	woman
dled	blenb	blach	black	wander	wowan
pled	dlend	black	bluck	wouder	womar
(bled)	blend	block	blick	wonder	woman
blad	blemb	blokc	block	wonber	moman

C **Find the missing letters. Then write the word.**

1. __b__ __l__ e d _____

2. ____ ____ e n d _____

3. b l o ____ ____ _____

© 2001 Steck-Vaughn Company. All Rights Reserved.

Name _____

3

Words with *bl-*

| bled | black | woman |
| block | blend | wonder |

A Fill in the boxes with the correct spelling words.

1. b l e n d

2.

3.

4.

5.

6.

B Fill in each blank with the correct spelling word.

1. A girl grows up to become a **woman**.
   woman   wonder

2. My foot _____ when I cut it.
   block   bled

3. Please _____ the yellow and blue paint.
   blend   bled

4. He writes with a _____ pen.
   black   block

5. I _____ if the movie has started.
   bled   wonder

6. Is your house on the same _____ as mine?
   block   bled

Words with *bl-*

bled	black	woman
block	blend	wonder

A Fill in each blank with a spelling word.

1. Will you _____ the sugar and flour together?

2. We asked the _____ to join our club.

3. Is there a new house on that _____?

B Find the hidden spelling words.

```
f  o  b  l  e  n  d  z
t  l  a  r  o  p  r  b
a  w  o  m  a  n  o  l
z  o  f  t  r  n  b  e
p  n  b  u  b  k  f  d
b  d  e  b  l  o  c  k
o  e  c  r  a  l  l  d
w  r  z  y  c  a  m  h
f  t  r  n  k  b  c  e
```

C Match each picture with its word. Then write the word.

1. block _____

2. woman _____

Name _____

© 2001 Steck-Vaughn Company. All Rights Reserved.

DAY
4

Words with *bl-*

bled	black	woman
block	blend	wonder

A Put an *X* on the word that is <u>not</u> the same.

1. blend	blend	blend	bl~~e~~nb	blend
2. bled	bled	bleb	bled	bled
3. woman	woman	woman	woman	wowan
4. block	black	block	block	block
5. wonder	wonder	wonden	wonder	wonder

B Complete each sentence.

1. The <u>black</u> clouds _____.

2. The <u>woman</u> went _____.

3. I <u>wonder</u> if _____.

C Use the correct spelling words to complete the story.

I was walking home when I felt some raindrops on my arm. I looked up at the sky, and I saw ____black____ clouds. All of a sudden it started to rain very hard. "I _____ if I can make it home since my house is on the next _____," I thought to myself. Then I saw my friend, Mrs. Jones. She asked me to come in her house and wait until the rain stopped.

Words with *gl-* and *fl-*

glad	flag	many
glass	flip	wash

A Circle the spelling word. Then write it on the line.

1. Can you flip those pancakes? _____

2. I need to wash the dishes. _____

3. She poured milk into a glass. _____

4. Are you glad that it is fall? _____

5. There is a flag in front of the building. _____

6. We can spell many new words. _____

B Circle the word that is the same as the top one.

glad	many	glass	flag	flip	wash
glod	mony	gloss	flag	flep	wish
glab	mary	glass	ftug	flop	wask
glad	mang	gluss	flog	flup	wash
glub	many	gliss	flng	flip	wosh

C Find the missing letters. Then write the word.

1. _____ _____ a d   _____

2. _____ l a g   _____

3. m _____ _____ y   _____

Name _____

© 2001 Steck-Vaughn Company. All Rights Reserved.

7

Words with *gl-* and *fl-*

DAY 2

glad	flag	many
glass	flip	wash

A Fill in the boxes with the correct spelling words.

1.

2.

3.

4.

5.

6.

B Fill in each blank with the correct spelling word.

1. The _____ has bright colors on it.
   flip   flag

2. He made lemonade in the _____ pitcher.
   glad   glass

3. My gym teacher helped me do a back _____.
   flip   flag

4. We _____ our car once a week.
   many   wash

5. I have so _____ books.
   many   wash

6. I'm _____ that today is Friday.
   glad   glass

Friday
14
October

Words with *gl-* and *fl-*

DAY 3

glad	flag	many
glass	flip	wash

A Use the correct spelling words to complete the story.

I like to pretend that I am a cowboy. I wake up when the

sun rises. I _____ pancakes over a campfire. I

_____ my plate in a stream.

Then I ride my horse for _____ hours. I work with

other cowboys. We take the cows up a trail. We have to

watch for storms and other kinds of trouble.

At night I sleep on the ground and watch the stars above.

I am _____ I'm a cowboy.

B Complete each sentence.

1. I am <u>glad</u> when _____.

2. There are <u>many</u> _____.

3. The <u>flag</u> almost _____.

C Write words that begin like each spelling word below.

<u>g</u>lad   <u>f</u>lag   <u>m</u>any   <u>w</u>ash

<u>glue</u>   _____   _____   _____

_____   _____   _____   _____

© 2001 Steck-Vaughn Company. All Rights Reserved.

Name _____

9

Words with *gl-* and *fl-*

DAY 4

glad	flag	many
glass	flip	wash

A Write each spelling word three times.

1. flag _____ _____ _____

2. wash _____ _____ _____

3. glad _____ _____ _____

4. many _____ _____ _____

5. glass _____ _____ _____

6. flip _____ _____ _____

B Match each word with its picture. Then write the word.

1. flip _____

2. glass _____

3. flag _____

C Put an X on the word that is <u>not</u> the same.

1. wash	wash	wask	wash	wash
2. flip	fliq	flip	flip	flip
3. glad	glad	glad	glad	glab

Words with *pl-* and *sl-*

DAY 1

plant	slept	small
plus	slid	try

A Circle the spelling word. Then write it on the line.

1. The car slid on the ice. _____

2. My sock has a small hole in it. _____

3. Two plus two is four. _____

4. He always remembers to water his plant. _____

5. I will try to meet you at the park. _____

6. We slept in a tent at camp. _____

B Find the missing letters. Then write the word.

1. p l _____ _____ _____   _____

2. _____ _____ e p t   _____

3. _____ m _____ _____ l   _____

C Use the correct spelling words to complete the story.

Last winter my family was driving across town. It was

snowing. Our car _____ on ice and hit a rock on the

side of the road. The car door got a _____ dent. We

were scared, but we were happy no one was hurt.

© 2001 Steck-Vaughn Company. All Rights Reserved.

Name _____

11

Words with *pl-* and *sl-*

plant	slept	small
plus	slid	try

A Circle the word that is the same as the top one.

plant	plus	try	slept	slid	small
dlant	blus	fry	slipt	sled	smell
plant	dlus	tny	slopt	slud	snell
olant	plus	try	slupt	slod	small
ptant	plos	try	slept	slid	swall

B Fill in each blank with the correct spelling word.

1. Seven _____ seven is fourteen.
   plant   plus

2. I _____ across the wet floor.
   slid   slept

3. You cannot do it unless you _____.
   try   small

4. My new kitten is _____.
   try   small

5. A corn _____ can grow to be very tall.
   plus   plant

6. I _____ in my new bed last night.
   slept   plant

DAY 3

Words with *pl-* and *sl-*

plant	slept	small
plus	slid	try

A **Fill in the boxes with the correct spelling words.**

1.

2.

3.

4.

5.

6.

B **Write the spelling words in ABC order.**

1. plant

2. plus

3. _____

4. _____

5. _____

6. _____

C **Find the hidden spelling words.**

```
e  n  o  g  s  r  v  x  t  w
v  a  b  p  l  a  n  t  i  n
e  i  p  r  e  g  r  o  w  l
p  l  u  s  p  x  t  l  a  b
f  l  i  r  t  s  s  l  i  d
b  c  d  t  f  m  g  h  j  k
l  m  n  r  p  a  q  r  s  t
v  w  a  y  e  l  i  o  u  y
r  b  i  t  d  l  p  a  t  g
```

© 2001 Steck-Vaughn Company. All Rights Reserved.

Name _____

13

Words with *pl-* and *sl-*

DAY
4

plant	slept	small
plus	slid	try

A Put an *X* on the word that is **not** the same.

1. slept	slept	slept	slcpt	slept
2. try	try	tny	try	try
3. slid	slib	slid	slid	slid
4. plant	plant	plant	plant	plart
5. small	snall	small	small	small
6. plus	plns	plus	plus	plus

B Complete each sentence.

1. I slept until _____.

2. The box slid _____.

C Write each spelling word three times.

1. slept _____ _____ _____

2. small _____ _____ _____

3. plus _____ _____ _____

4. try _____ _____ _____

5. slid _____ _____ _____

6. plant _____ _____ _____

DAY
1

Words with *sc-* and *scr-*

scalp	scrub	plenty
scan	scrap	brown

A **Circle the spelling word. Then write it on the line.**

1. Please scrub when you clean the tub. _____

2. Do you have brown eyes? _____

3. Your hair grows from your scalp. _____

4. We have plenty of food in the house. _____

5. Scan the page to find the answer. _____

6. I wrote the note on a scrap of paper. _____

B **Find the missing letters. Then write the word.**

1. _____ _____ _____ u b   _____

2. _____ _____ a l p   _____

3. s c _____ _____ _____   _____

C **Circle the word that is the same as the top one.**

scalp	brown	scan	plenty	scrap	scrub
scald	brawn	scan	planty	scrab	scrud
scalb	brown	scar	plemty	serap	serub
scalp	bnown	sear	plenyt	scrap	scnub
sealp	bromn	scon	plenty	srcap	scrub

© 2001 Steck-Vaughn Company. All Rights Reserved.

Name _____

15

Words with *sc-* and *scr-*

scalp	scrub	plenty
scan	scrap	brown

A Find the hidden spelling words.

```
n  w  o  z  f  t  u  g  a  l
t  r  m  s  c  a  l  p  s  s
b  s  c  a  n  m  n  g  h  f
s  c  r  a  p  b  l  e  r  n
c  r  p  q  p  r  f  g  p  v
p  u  r  s  l  o  z  w  n  g
u  b  t  u  e  w  p  r  s  g
b  l  c  n  n  n  i  n  g  o
r  r  v  p  t  n  f  r  o  p
s  a  l  p  y  r  f  g  p  v
f  m  n  g  h  o  z  w  n  g
```

B Fill in each blank with a spelling word.

1. _____ the page for the correct answer.

2. A small piece of food is a _____.

3. You must _____ the floor to clean it.

C Write the spelling words in ABC order.

1. _____   2. _____   3. _____

4. _____   5. _____   6. _____

DAY
3

Words with *sc-* and *scr-*

scalp	scrub	plenty
scan	scrap	brown

A Fill in each blank with the correct spelling word.

1. Do you _____ the sink after you wash dishes?
   scalp   scrub

2. The color of the dog's fur is _____.
   scan   brown

3. I will pick every _____ of paper off the floor.
   scrap   scalp

4. I like _____ of cheese on pizza.
   plenty   scan

5. Your _____ can itch if your hair is not clean.
   scrub   scalp

B Write the spelling word that rhymes with the word group.

1. down   gown   frown   _____

2. sub   cub   tub   _____

3. man   ran   can   _____

C Write these spelling words from other lessons.

1. many _____   2. flag _____

3. wash _____   4. plus _____

© 2001 Steck-Vaughn Company. All Rights Reserved.

Name _____

17

DAY 4

Words with *sc-* and *scr-*

scalp	scrub	plenty
scan	scrap	brown

A **Put an *X* on the word that is _not_ the same.**

1.	scrap	scrap	serap	scrap	scrap
2.	plenty	plenty	plenty	planty	plenty
3.	scan	scar	scan	scan	scan
4.	scrub	scrub	scrub	scrud	scrub
5.	scalp	scalp	scalp	scalp	scolp
6.	brown	brown	broun	brown	brown

B **Complete each sentence.**

1. The hair on my scalp is _____.

2. I scan the newspaper for _____.

C **Use the correct spelling words to complete the story.**

Next week my friends are coming to visit me. I have a few

things to do around my house before they arrive.

First, I must clean the kitchen. I will need to be sure to use

_____ of soap and hot water when I _____

the sink. Next, I need to clean every room in the house. If I

find one _____ of trash, I will throw it away.

Words with *sk-* and *sn-*

DAY 1

skill	snap	flute
skunk	snack	goes

A Circle the spelling word. Then write it on the line.

1. A skunk is a black and white animal. _____

2. She can play the flute. _____

3. Can you snap your fingers? _____

4. He goes to his piano lesson every day. _____

5. Do you eat a snack before lunch? _____

6. It takes a lot of skill to play basketball well. _____

B Use the correct spelling words to complete the story.

The girl really wanted to learn a new _____.

"I think I'll learn how to play the _____," she said.

She bought a flute and a book for beginners. She thought

playing the flute would be a _____.

But it wasn't easy. She had trouble learning the notes in

the book. "Maybe I should take lessons," she thought. The girl

found a teacher. Soon she played the flute very well.

C Write the spelling word that rhymes with the word pair.

crack   back   _____

© 2001 Steck-Vaughn Company. All Rights Reserved.

Name _____

19

Words with *sk-* and *sn-*

DAY 2

skill	snap	flute
skunk	snack	goes

A Fill in each blank with the correct spelling word.

1. Can you _____ your fingers?
   snap   snack

2. A _____ has a white stripe down its back.
   skill   skunk

3. It takes _____ to do well at any sport.
   skill   skunk

4. I love to play the _____.
   goes   flute

5. She often _____ to the lake.
   snap   goes

6. Do you eat a _____ between meals?
   snack   snap

B Find the missing letters. Then write the word.

_____ _____ i l l   _____

C Write the spelling words in ABC order.

1. _____   2. _____   3. _____

4. _____   5. _____   6. _____

Lesson 5 — Words with *sk-* and *sn-*

DAY 3

skill	snap	flute
skunk	snack	goes

A Fill in the boxes with the correct spelling words.

1.

2.

3.

4.

5.

6.

B Fill in each blank with a spelling word.

1. It takes _____ to sing well.

2. The _____ smells very bad.

3. Would you like a _____ to eat?

C Match each word with its picture. Then write the word.

1. snack   _____

2. flute   _____

3. snap   _____

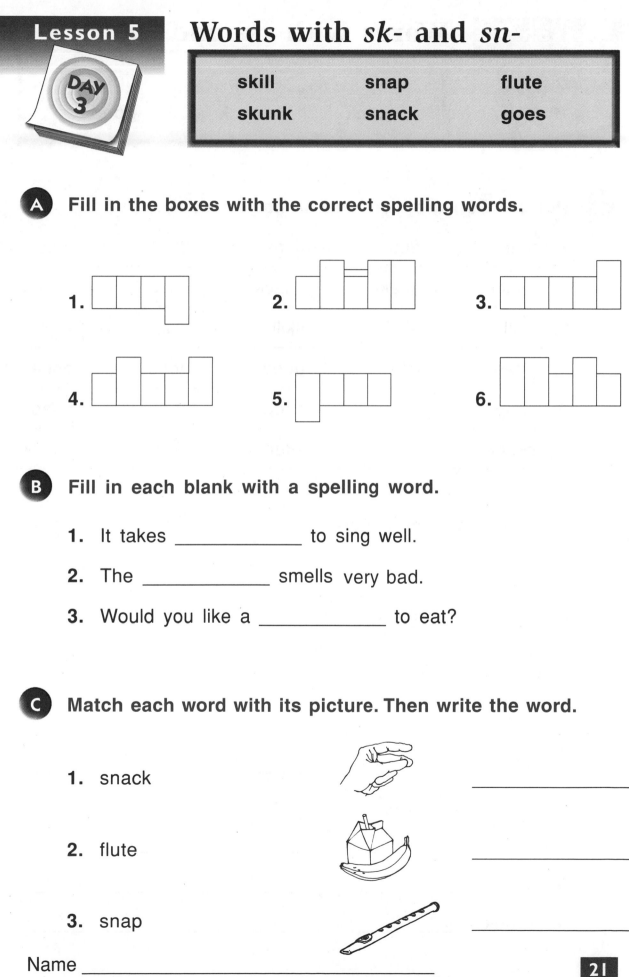

Name _____

© 2001 Steck-Vaughn Company. All Rights Reserved.

Lesson 5

Words with *sk-* and *sn-*

skill	snap	flute
skunk	snack	goes

 A Put an *X* on the word that is <u>not</u> the same.

1. flute	flute	flute	fluet	flute
2. snack	snake	snack	snack	snack
3. skill	shill	skill	skill	skill
4. goes	goes	goes	goes	gose
5. snap	snap	snop	snap	snap
6. skunk	skunk	skunk	sknuk	skunk

B Complete each sentence.

1. The <u>skunk</u> _____.

2. My favorite <u>snack</u> is _____.

C Write each spelling word three times.

1. flute _____ _____ _____

2. snack _____ _____ _____

3. skill _____ _____ _____

4. snap _____ _____ _____

5. goes _____ _____ _____

6. skunk _____ _____ _____

Review

scan	flute	goes
bled	flag	wash
glad	plant	slept
woman	flip	glass
plus	snack	wonder

A Match each picture with its word. Then write the word.

1. flag _____

2. woman _____

3. flute _____

B Fill in each blank with the correct spelling word.

1. I cut my finger and it _____.
   bled   goes

2. Popcorn is my favorite _____ food.
   scan   snack

3. Four _____ five is nine.
   plus   plant

4. Are you _____ that today is Friday?
   glass   glad

   Friday
   14
   October

5. I _____ how I did on my math test.
   wonder   woman

Name _____

© 2001 Steck-Vaughn Company. All Rights Reserved.

23

small	snap	scalp
skill	black	blend
many	plenty	skunk
scrap	block	brown
scrub	slid	try

C **Find the missing letters. Then write the word.**

1. ____ ____ ____ a p _____

2. ____ ____ e n d _____

3. s l ____ ____ _____

4. b r ____ ____ ____ _____

5. s ____ ____ ____ b _____

6. ____ ____ o c k _____

7. ____ ____ a l p _____

D **Use the correct spelling words to complete the story.**

Have you ever tried to get near a _____? I have

seen skunks _____ times, but I have never been close

to one. I _____ and try, but nothing works. I have

walked up to _____ of skunks on my tiptoes. I never

say a word, though. Every time, a twig will _____

under my feet, or I will make a noise that scares them off.

Those _____ and white animals always get away!

Lesson 6 Words with *sp-* and *st-*

DAY 1

spend	study	never
spill	stamp	warm

A Circle the spelling word. Then write it on the line.

1. Do not forget to study your spelling. _____

2. He never forgets to bring his wallet. _____

3. I have a few dollars to spend. _____

4. I need to put a stamp on my letter. _____

5. The man tried not to spill his tea. _____

6. Always wear warm clothes on cold days. _____

B Use the correct spelling words to complete the story.

Let's try to _____ fifteen minutes each night

working on spelling words. We'll work at our desks.

We can _____ best in our own rooms. We should

_____ work in front of the TV.

C Write these spelling words from other lessons.

1. scrub _____   2. black _____

3. scrap _____   4. snap _____

5. snack _____   6. skunk _____

7. scalp _____   8. brown _____

© 2001 Steck-Vaughn Company. All Rights Reserved.

Name _____

Words with *sp-* and *st-*

DAY 2

spend	study	never
spill	stamp	warm

A Fill in each blank with the correct spelling word.

1. How do you _____ your spelling words?

stamp   study

2. When you fill the car with gas, try not to _____

spend   spill

any.

3. I hope I _____ eat seven hot dogs again!

never   spend

4. If you don't _____ all your money, you can save some.

spend   warm

5. We like to be outside on _____ days.

warm   stamp

B Find the hidden spelling words.

```
y   d   s   t   u   d   y   r
q   i   p   m   a   g   r   o
s   d   i   z   r   o   o   b
m   w   l   s   p   e   n   d
f   a   l   t   p   q   e   e
g   r   b   a   r   b   v   r
l   m   q   m   o   c   e   j
h   i   f   p   p   d   r   z
```

Words with *sp-* and *st-*

spend	study	never
spill	stamp	warm

A Find the missing letters. Then write the word.

1. _____ _____ e n d   _____

2. s p _____ _____ _____   _____

B Write the spelling words in ABC order.

1. _____   2. _____   3. _____

4. _____   5. _____   6. _____

C Write words that begin like each spelling word below.

spend   stamp   never   warm

_____ _____ _____ _____

_____ _____ _____ _____

D Fill in the boxes with the correct spelling words.

1.

2.

3.

4.

5.

6.

© 2001 Steck-Vaughn Company. All Rights Reserved.

Name _____

27

Words with *sp-* and *st-*

spend	study	never
spill	stamp	warm

A **Complete each sentence.**

1. Sometimes I spill _____.

2. It is warm _____.

3. I like to spend my time _____.

B **Circle the word that is the same as the top one.**

stamp	warm	study	spend	never	spill
stump	warw	stady	spend	rever	spell
stawp	marm	stuyd	sperd	never	sqill
stamp	worm	study	spenb	newer	sgill
sfump	warm	sludy	speud	neven	spill

C **Write each spelling word three times.**

1. spill _____ _____ _____

2. never _____ _____ _____

3. stamp _____ _____ _____

4. study _____ _____ _____

5. spend _____ _____ _____

6. warm _____ _____ _____

DAY 1

Words with *sw-*

swing	swimming	book
swim	arm	four

A **Circle the spelling word. Then write it on the line.**

1. Monkeys like to swing from tree to tree. _____

2. She has read that book three times. _____

3. Two plus two is four. _____

4. Do you know how to swim? _____

5. I broke my arm when I fell. _____

6. Swimming is fun. _____

B **Write the spelling word that rhymes with the word pair.**

1. sing   thing   _____

2. farm   charm   _____

3. look   took   _____

4. dim   rim   _____

C **Use the correct spelling words to complete the story.**

The twins had a fun summer. On their birthday in June,

they were given a _____ set for their backyard. They

spent almost every day _____ in their friend's pool. In

July, they spent _____ weeks on a farm.

© 2001 Steck-Vaughn Company. All Rights Reserved.

Name _____

Lesson 7

Words with *sw-*

swing	swimming	book
swim	arm	four

A Fill in each blank with the correct spelling word.

1. Let's go _____ at the pool.
   arm   swimming

2. I want to read a _____ about jets.
   swim   book

3. It's fun to _____ when it's hot.
   swim   book

4. We vote for a president every _____ years.
   book   four

5. My sister broke her _____.
   arm   swimming

6. My dad made a _____ to play on.
   swing   book

B Write the spelling words in ABC order.

1. _____   2. _____   3. _____

4. _____   5. _____   6. _____

C Fill in the blank with a spelling word.

I went for a _____ in the pool.

Lesson 7

Words with *sw-*

swing	swimming	book
swim	arm	four

 A Find the hidden spelling words.

```
p  s  e  r  n  a  g  z  a
s  w  i  n  g  b  o  o  k
w  i  a  t  r  f  o  o  o
i  m  a  v  m  g  d  t  m
m  m  f  o  u  r  r  z  k
u  i  i  e  f  z  n  c  t
o  n  b  e  a  b  o  u  t
i  g  e  n  a  r  m  s  o
```

B Fill in the boxes with the correct spelling words.

1.
2.
3.

4.
5.
6.

C Write these spelling words from other lessons.

1. woman _____   2. glass _____

3. plant _____   4. scalp _____

5. snack _____   6. study _____

Name _____

© 2001 Steck-Vaughn Company. All Rights Reserved.

DAY 4

Words with *sw-*

swing	swimming	book
swim	arm	four

A Write each spelling word three times.

1. swim _____ _____ _____

2. swimming _____ _____ _____

3. swing _____ _____ _____

4. arm _____ _____ _____

5. four _____ _____ _____

6. book _____ _____ _____

B Circle the word that is the same as the top one.

arm	book	swim	swimming	four	swing
ram	booh	swin	smimming	foun	swing
amr	dook	swim	snimming	tour	swirg
mar	book	smim	swimming	fonr	swinq
arm	boak	swiw	swimmimg	four	sming

C Complete each sentence.

1. Your <u>arm</u> is _____.

2. My new <u>book</u> is _____.

3. I can eat <u>four</u> _____.

Words with *cr-*

crust	crash	much
crack	myself	kind

A Circle the spelling word. Then write it on the line.

1. Two cars were in a crash. _____

2. The boy is kind to his dog. _____

3. I try to do nice things for myself. _____

4. The crust on this pie tastes good. _____

5. I do not like liver very much. _____

6. There is a crack in the mirror. _____

B Use the correct spelling words to complete the story.

I always try to be helpful and _____ to people. If I

see someone carrying something heavy, I offer to help carry it.

If I open a door and someone is behind me, I hold the door

open until the person walks through. When my mom makes a

cherry pie for me, I tell her that my favorite part of the pie is

the _____. That always makes my mom smile.

And of course, I never forget to be kind to _____.

When you are nice, you feel _____ better about

yourself.

© 2001 Steck-Vaughn Company. All Rights Reserved.

Name _____

Words with *cr-*

crust	crash	much
crack	myself	kind

A **Fill in each blank with the correct spelling word.**

1. I bought the apple _____.
   myself   much

2. She made a pie with a beautiful _____.
   crust   crack

3. A rock hit the window and made a _____ in it.
   crust   crack

4. The car and truck were in a _____.
   crack   crash

B **Write the spelling words in ABC order.**

1. _____   2. _____   3. _____

4. _____   5. _____   6. _____

C **Find the hidden spelling words.**

```
f  m  a  b  b  k  i  n  g  h
m  u  f  b  r  i  n  g  e  c
p  c  f  s  i  n  r  o  v  r
a  h  g  h  c  d  j  o  k  a
c  r  a  c  k  o  o  d  a  s
p  r  c  r  u  s  t  o  s  h
z  o  m  y  s  e  l  f  b  s
```

Words with *cr-*

DAY 3

crust	crash	much
crack	myself	kind

A **Fill in the boxes with the correct spelling words.**

1.

2.

3.

4.

5.

6.

B **Find the missing letters. Then write the word.**

1. m _____ _____ h _____

2. m y _____ _____ _____ _____ _____

3. _____ _____ u s t _____

C **Circle the word that is the same as the top one.**

crust	crash	much	crack	kind	myself
crusf	crush	nuch	crack	kird	myselt
cnust	crash	muck	cnack	kirb	myself
crost	crask	much	cvack	kind	mgself
crust	crahs	mnck	crach	kinb	myself

© 2001 Steck-Vaughn Company. All Rights Reserved.

Name _____

Words with *cr-*

crust	crash	much
crack	myself	kind

DAY 4

A **Match each word with its picture. Then write the word.**

1. crust _____

2. myself _____

3. crack _____

B **Complete each sentence.**

1. I like <u>myself</u> when _____.

2. Be <u>kind</u> _____.

C **Write each spelling word three times.**

1. myself _____ _____ _____

2. kind _____ _____ _____

3. much _____ _____ _____

4. crash _____ _____ _____

5. crack _____ _____ _____

6. crust _____ _____ _____

DAY 1

Words with *dr-* and *gr-*

drum	grass	frog
drink	grab	done

A Circle the spelling word. Then write it on the line.

1. It's good to drink milk. _____

2. That frog makes funny noises at night. _____

3. The cookies are almost done. _____

4. Many bands have a bass drum. _____

5. Try to grab the doorknob. _____

6. In the winter the grass turns brown. _____

B Use the correct spelling words to complete the story.

One sunny afternoon, my friend and I took a picnic lunch

down by the lake. We sat on a dock near some tall

_____. While we talked, we ate our peanut butter

crackers and drank tea.

Loud sounds came from the tall grass. Then we saw

something jump. It was a _____! I wanted to keep the

frog for a pet, so I tried to _____ it. But the frog

hopped away. We never saw it again, but we still go to the

lake to look for it.

© 2001 Steck-Vaughn Company. All Rights Reserved.

Name _____

Words with *dr-* and *gr-*

drum	grass	frog
drink	grab	done

A Fill in each blank with the correct spelling word.

1. Do you like to _____ milk?
   grab   drink

2. I like to hear _____ noises at night.
   grass   frog

3. What kind of _____ would you like to play?
   drum   done

4. I mow the _____ in my yard.
   drink   grass

5. Have you _____ something nice for someone today?
   drum   done

6. Please _____ those papers that are falling!
   grab   drink

B Find the hidden spelling words.

```
d z f g r a s s
o d r i n k p o
n r o g h h r d
e u g r e a f l
n m i a p v n v
p r p b e e o e
```

DAY 3

Words with *dr-* and *gr-*

drum	grass	frog
drink	grab	done

A Find the missing letters. Then write the word.

1. _____ _____ u m   _____

2. _____ _____ o g   _____

3. d _____ n _____   _____

B Write the spelling words in ABC order.

1. _____   2. _____   3. _____

4. _____   5. _____   6. _____

C Circle the word that is the same as the top one.

grab	drum	done	grass	frog	drink
qrab	brum	bone	grass	trog	drinh
grad	druw	dore	qrass	frog	drirk
grab	drnm	done	gnass	froq	brink
gnab	drum	donc	graas	frug	drink

D Complete each sentence.

1. I put a <u>frog</u> _____.

2. Don't <u>grab</u> the _____.

© 2001 Steck-Vaughn Company. All Rights Reserved.

Name _____

39

Words with *dr-* and *gr-*

drum	grass	frog
drink	grab	done

A Match each picture with its word. Then write the word.

1. drink _____

2. frog _____

3. drum _____

B Fill in the boxes with the correct spelling words.

1.

2.

3.

4.

5.

6.

C Write each spelling word three times.

1. drink _____ _____ _____

2. grass _____ _____ _____

3. frog _____ _____ _____

4. done _____ _____ _____

5. grab _____ _____ _____

Words with *pr-* and *str-*

DAY 1

prompt	string	group
press	strap	laugh

A Circle the spelling word. Then write it on the line.

1. You use an iron to press your clothes. _____

2. We flew a kite on a long string. _____

3. Stay with our group on the field trip. _____

4. If you are on time, you are prompt. _____

5. A good teacher knows how to laugh. _____

6. My purse has a strap to hold on to. _____

B Write the spelling word that rhymes with the word pair.

1. mess   dress   _____

2. wing   sing   _____

3. lap   nap   _____

C Complete each sentence.

1. I like to <u>laugh</u> at _____.

2. I use a <u>string</u> _____.

D Find the missing letters. Then write the word.

1. _____ _____ o m _____ t   _____

2. _____ _____ _____ g h   _____

© 2001 Steck-Vaughn Company. All Rights Reserved.

Name _____

Words with *pr-* and *str-*

DAY 2

prompt	**string**	**group**
press	**strap**	**laugh**

A Fill in each blank with the correct spelling word.

1. Fly the kite on a _____.
   string   strap

2. They are in my singing _____.
   group   press

3. Use an iron to _____ wrinkled clothes.
   group   press

4. The purse has a shoulder _____.
   string   strap

5. You are a _____ person if you are on time.
   prompt   laugh

B Write words that begin like each spelling word below.

group   press   string   laugh

_____   _____   _____   _____

_____   _____   _____   _____

C Write the spelling words in ABC order.

1. _____   2. _____   3. _____

4. _____   5. _____   6. _____

DAY 3

Words with *pr-* and *str-*

prompt	string	group
press	strap	laugh

A Use the correct spelling words to complete the story.

Next weekend, my friends and I are going to the park. We plan to fly kites all day. We need to be _____ and meet by 8:00 A.M. so that we can leave by 8:15. Someone will need to bring extra _____. Last year we didn't have enough!

There's not a place to buy food or drinks at the park, so we can't forget to take our lunches. We have to be ready so our _____ can have fun!

B Write each spelling word two times in cursive.

laugh _____

press _____

string _____

strap _____

group _____

prompt _____

C Which spelling word ends with an *f* sound? _____

© 2001 Steck-Vaughn Company. All Rights Reserved.

Name _____

43

Words with *pr-* and *str-*

DAY 4

prompt	string	group
press	strap	laugh

A Fill in the boxes with the correct spelling words.

1.
2.
3.
4.
5.
6.

B Write these spelling words from other lessons.

1. crust _____

2. myself _____

3. crack _____

4. drum _____

5. frog _____

6. drink _____

C Write each spelling word three times.

1. strap _____ _____ _____

2. laugh _____ _____ _____

3. press _____ _____ _____

4. group _____ _____ _____

5. string _____ _____ _____

6. prompt _____ _____ _____

Review _____

book	swing	crack
stamp	swimming	crash
study	swim	frog
four	crust	grass
spill	spend	warm

A **Match each picture with its word. Then write the word.**

1. swing _____

2. crack _____

3. frog _____

B **Fill in each blank with the correct spelling word.**

1. How much did you _____ on lunch?
    spill   spend

2. I cut our _____ in the summer.
    grass   press

3. We enjoy _____ spring weather.
    warm   swim

4. How long did you _____ for the spelling test?
    stamp   study

5. This apple pie _____ tastes great!
    crash   crust

Name _____

© 2001 Steck-Vaughn Company. All Rights Reserved.

Review

arm	drink	kind
much	prompt	done
string	press	myself
strap	grab	never
drum	group	laugh

C Find the missing letters. Then write the word.

1. _____ r _____ _____ s   _____

2. d r _____ _____ _____   _____

3. _____ _____ _____ g h   _____

4. s t r _____ _____ _____   _____

5. p r _____ _____ _____ _____   _____

6. k _____ _____ _____   _____

7. d _____ _____ e   _____

D Use the correct spelling words to complete the story.

When I get ready to play the _____ in the marching

band, it takes me forever! First, I have to get my drum. Then I hook

it to a _____ that goes around my neck and under my

right _____. Next, I pick up my drum sticks. Finally, I join

the rest of the _____ that plays in the band.

I'm always the last one to get ready. But I enjoy playing the

drum too _____ to change to an easier instrument.

Words with *tr-* and *cl-*

| trip | club | again |
| trust | class | after |

A Circle the spelling word. Then write it on the line.

1. Do you belong to the stamp club? _____

2. Our group took a trip to the beach. _____

3. I trust you to keep a secret. _____

4. Are you in my dance class? _____

5. Will you take me surfing again? _____

6. We will leave for the store after lunch. _____

B Use the correct spelling words to complete the story.

_____ lunch on Friday, our science _____ will visit the zoo. We are taking a bus there. We plan to take many pictures on our _____. We hope to see snakes, bears, and lions. I hear they have a monkey island. It will really be fun!

C Write the spelling words in ABC order.

1. _____ 2. _____ 3. _____

4. _____ 5. _____ 6. _____

© 2001 Steck-Vaughn Company. All Rights Reserved.

Name _____

Words with *tr-* and *cl-*

trip	club	again
trust	class	after

A Fill in each blank with the correct spelling word.

1. We would like to join a biking _____.

trust   club

2. I _____ you to do the right thing.

trust   trip

3. How many ladies are in our art _____ ?

class   trip

4. Please sing each line _____ me.

again   after

5. Let's sing the song _____.

again   after

6. Our family takes a _____ together every summer.

trust   trip

B Write the spelling word that rhymes with the word pair.

1. lip   rip   _____

2. rub   tub   _____

3. dust   rust   _____

4. grass   pass   _____

5. rafter   laughter   _____

Words with *tr-* and *cl-*

trip	club	again
trust	class	after

A Find the hidden spelling words.

```
r  s  o  m  e  b  o  d  y  e  s
a  f  m  u  a  t  r  i  p  o  p
f  a  n  p  g  r  o  c  a  c  e
t  t  o  o  a  u  d  a  r  l  d
e  e  n  p  i  s  e  a  t  a  o
r  i  r  e  n  t  a  o  y  s  e
g  s  c  l  u  b  o  o  p  s  t
o  f  a  m  i  l  y  s  s  e  a
```

B Find the missing letters. Then write the word.

c _____ _____ s _____   _____

C Write each spelling word three times.

1. club   _____ _____ _____

2. class   _____ _____ _____

3. trip   _____ _____ _____

4. trust   _____ _____ _____

5. again   _____ _____ _____

6. after   _____ _____ _____

© 2001 Steck-Vaughn Company. All Rights Reserved.

Name _____

Words with *tr-* and *cl-*

DAY 4

trip	club	again
trust	class	after

A Put an *X* on the word that is <u>not</u> the same.

1.	trip	trip	trip	trap	trip
2.	club	club	clab	club	club
3.	trust	trusf	trust	trust	trust
4.	class	class	class	class	calss
5.	again	again	again	aigan	again
6.	after	after	atfer	after	after

B Write each spelling word two times in cursive.

club

class

after

again

trip

trust

C Which spelling word has three vowels? _____

Words with -*ank*, -*unk*, and -*nch*

DAY 1

drank	trunk	inch
bank	junk	pinch

A **Circle the spelling word. Then write it on the line.**

1. I drank three glasses of tea today. _____

2. That bug is at least an inch long. _____

3. I put my money in the bank. _____

4. We keep winter clothes in a trunk. _____

5. Be careful, that crab can pinch you. _____

6. This attic is full of junk. _____

B **Fill in each blank with the correct spelling word.**

1. The recipe called for a _____ of salt.
   trunk   pinch

2. If you save all that _____, you'll have to throw it
   inch   junk
   away later.

3. A safe place for your money is the _____.
   bank   pinch

4. The candle wick is about an _____ long.
   inch   pinch

5. An elephant has a long _____.
   drank   trunk

6. The big dog _____ all the water.
   drank   bank

© 2001 Steck-Vaughn Company. All Rights Reserved.

Name _____

Words with -*ank*, -*unk*, and -*nch*

DAY 2

drank	trunk	inch
bank	junk	pinch

A Write the spelling words in ABC order.

1. _____ 2. _____ 3. _____

4. _____ 5. _____ 6. _____

B Use the correct spelling words to complete the story.

   Last week I helped my brother move. We packed his things

in my car _____. Most of it was _____! He

doesn't like to throw anything away. There wasn't even an

_____ of space left in my trunk. Maybe we'll find a

surprise in all that junk.

C Find the hidden spelling words.

```
n  b  c  r  e  e  l  s  o  j
a  b  c  t  u  b  a  y  s  u
w  b  c  p  b  a  d  o  w  n
p  r  o  s  a  t  r  u  n  k
i  n  c  h  a  s  a  n  a  p
n  b  c  a  s  k  n  o  w  m
c  a  r  b  a  n  k  n  e  e
h  z  q  e  y  u  i  s  e  e
r  t  v  e  s  t  d  f  o  r
```

Words with -*ank*, -*unk*, and -*nch*

drank	trunk	inch
bank	junk	pinch

A Write the spelling word that rhymes with the word pair.

1. finch   inch   _____

2. bunk   junk   _____

3. bank   rank   _____

B Find the missing letters. Then write the word.

1. _____ _____ c h   _____

2. _____ _____ u n k   _____

C Write each spelling word two times in cursive.

bank _____

drank _____

trunk _____

junk _____

inch _____

pinch _____

D Which spelling word begins with a vowel? _____

© 2001 Steck-Vaughn Company. All Rights Reserved.

Name _____

Words with *-ank, -unk,* and *-nch*

drank	trunk	inch
bank	junk	pinch

A Write each spelling word three times.

1. inch _____ _____ _____

2. pinch _____ _____ _____

3. drank _____ _____ _____

4. bank _____ _____ _____

5. trunk _____ _____ _____

6. junk _____ _____ _____

B Circle the word that is the same as the top one.

inch	drank	bank	pinch	trunk	junk
inck	brank	dank	piuch	trank	jank
irch	drink	bank	pinck	trink	jonk
inch	drunk	dunk	pinch	trnnk	junk
iuch	drank	bunk	pirch	trunk	jnnk

C Fill in the boxes with the correct spelling words.

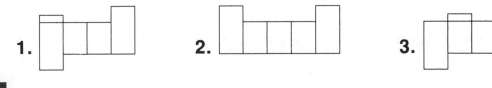

1.　　　　　2.　　　　　3.

Words with *-anch* and *-ung*

DAY 1

| branch | swung | together |
| ranch | strung | today |

A Circle the spelling word. Then write it on the line.

1. We strung the beads on this thread. _____

2. Cows and horses can live on a ranch. _____

3. Our family spends time together. _____

4. The monkey swung from the tree. _____

5. The leaves are still on the branch. _____

6. What are we having for lunch today? _____

B Fill in each blank with the correct spelling word.

1. We _____ a clothesline from the house to the garage.
   ranch   strung

2. I rode a horse on the _____.
   branch   ranch

3. Let's do our work _____ instead of tomorrow.
   together   today

4. I like to put puzzles _____.
   together   today

5. The door _____ open because of the strong wind.
   swung   ranch

6. The wind blew the _____ off the tree.
   branch   strung

© 2001 Steck-Vaughn Company. All Rights Reserved.

Name _____

Words with *-anch* and *-ung*

DAY 2

branch	swung	together
ranch	strung	today

A Write words that end like each spelling word below.

sw<u>ung</u>   to<u>day</u>   ra<u>nch</u>

_____   _____   _____

_____   _____   _____

B Use the correct spelling words to complete the story.

I went to the park _____ with my best friend. We
had a great time.

First, we _____ on the swings and went down the
slide. Then we saw a big tree _____ lying across
the creek. We walked across the branch. Then we were really
brave and walked backwards on the branch. We laughed so
hard that we fell in the creek! The water wasn't deep, though.
We always have fun _____.

C Write these spelling words from other lessons.

1. trust _____   **2.** again _____

3. inch _____   **4.** drank _____

5. junk _____   **6.** pinch _____

DAY 3

Words with *-anch* and *-ung*

branch	swung	together
ranch	strung	today

A Write words that begin like each spelling word below.

<u>sw</u>ung   <u>str</u>ung   <u>br</u>anch   <u>r</u>anch

_____ _____ _____ _____

_____ _____ _____ _____

_____ _____ _____ _____

B Find the missing letters. Then write the word.

1. ____ ____ ____ c h   _____

2. s w ____ ____ ____   _____

3. b r ____ ____ ____ h   _____

C Write each spelling word three times.

1. branch _____ _____ _____

2. ranch _____ _____ _____

3. swung _____ _____ _____

4. strung _____ _____ _____

5. together _____ _____ _____

6. today _____ _____ _____

© 2001 Steck-Vaughn Company. All Rights Reserved.

Name _____

Words with -*anch* and -*ung*

branch	swung	together
ranch	strung	today

A   Write each spelling word two times in cursive.

together _____

swung _____

strung _____

today _____

ranch _____

branch _____

B   Circle the word that is the same as the top one.

branch	ranch	swung	strung	today	together
brunch	ranch	smung	stnung	tobay	toqrther
bnarch	rench	swnng	strumg	foday	together
branch	ranck	swuug	stnnng	todag	togefher
brank	rauch	swung	strung	today	togethen

C   Complete each sentence.

1. The <u>ranch</u> is _____.

2. <u>Today</u> I'm going to _____.

58

Lesson 14 — Words with *-ink* and *-ar*

DAY 1

wink	collar	full
blink	dollar	hurt

A Circle the spelling word. Then write it on the line.

1. How many times do your eyes blink? _____

2. The basket was full of clean clothes. _____

3. The dog has a collar. _____

4. The candy bar costs a dollar. _____

5. If I wink, I'm playing a trick. _____

6. He did not hurt his foot. _____

B Fill in each blank with the correct spelling word.

1. Can you _____ with just one eye?
   full   wink

2. The dog's _____ is too big.
   dollar   collar

3. Does this pie cost more than a _____?
   full   dollar

4. When your eyes are tired, they sometimes _____.
   blink   dollar

5. The bowl is _____ of fresh fruit.
   hurt   full

6. The cut on my hand does not _____ now.
   hurt   full

© 2001 Steck-Vaughn Company. All Rights Reserved.

Name _____

Words with *-ink* and *-ar*

DAY 2

wink	collar	full
blink	dollar	hurt

A Find the hidden spelling words.

```
s  d  o  r  e  b  y  b  f  d  c  p
l  o  m  o  v  s  m  f  u  m  o  r
e  l  a  w  i  n  k  a  l  l  l  x
e  l  k  i  b  g  e  v  l  u  l  n
p  a  a  n  l  i  y  a  m  s  a  o
h  r  n  g  i  n  g  y  h  u  r  t
o  p  d  o  n  g  u  m  e  w  f  i
r  l  s  e  k  r  e  a  r  e  t  p
```

B Fill in the boxes with the correct spelling words.

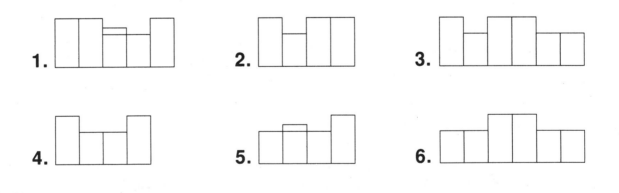

1.   2.   3.

4.   5.   6.

C Write these spelling words from other lessons.

1. trust _____

2. class _____

3. drank _____

4. pinch _____

60

DAY 3

Words with *-ink* and *-ar*

wink	collar	full
blink	dollar	hurt

A **Use the correct spelling words to complete the story.**

My dog Wags was playing outside. Wags was on his leash,

but he slipped out of his _____. He ran down the

sidewalk in front of our house. Then he ran toward the street.

Our street is usually _____ of cars, but only one

was coming this time. The driver saw Wags and stopped his

car. I was so happy that Wags was not _____!

B **Find the missing letters. Then write the word.**

f _____ _____ _____   _____

C **Write each spelling word three times.**

1. blink   _____ _____ _____

2. collar   _____ _____ _____

3. full   _____ _____ _____

4. hurt   _____ _____ _____

5. wink   _____ _____ _____

6. dollar   _____ _____ _____

© 2001 Steck-Vaughn Company. All Rights Reserved.

Name _____

Words with -*ink* and -*ar*

wink	**collar**	**full**
blink	**dollar**	**hurt**

A Write each spelling word two times in cursive.

wink _____

full _____

collar _____

dollar _____

hurt _____

blink _____

B Circle the word that is the same as the top one.

collar	wink	hurt	full	dollar	blink
collur	winh	burt	tull	dollar	blinh
coller	wirk	hunt	full	doller	dlink
coler	wink	hurt	fnll	dallor	blink
collar	wiuk	bunt	foll	dollur	blirk

C Complete each sentence.

1. It can <u>hurt</u> when _____.

2. I paid a <u>dollar</u> for _____.

Words with *th-*

these	think	pretty
those	thank	eight

DAY 1

A Circle the spelling word. Then write it on the line.

1. Thank you for the gift. _____

2. You look pretty in your new dress. _____

3. Please hand me those papers. _____

4. How old do you think I am? _____

5. Eight eggs are left in the nest. _____

6. I like these jeans on the rack next to me. _____

B Fill in each blank with the correct spelling word.

1. I want one of _____ apples over there.
   these   those

2. _____ people went swimming.
   Eight   Think

3. Who do you _____ will win the game?
   thank   think

4. I want to _____ you for my gift.
   thank   think

5. May I give you one of _____ flowers?
   these   pretty

6. The blue sky looked so _____!
   these   pretty

© 2001 Steck-Vaughn Company. All Rights Reserved.

Name _____

63

Words with *th-*

these	think	pretty
those	thank	eight

A Write the spelling words in ABC order.

1. _____ 2. _____ 3. _____

4. _____ 5. _____ 6. _____

B Find the hidden spelling words.

```
a  u  a  d  l  a  o  n  e
i  t  s  b  e  a  r  t  o
t  h  e  s  e  r  e  h  e
a  e  a  l  l  a  r  o  t
e  i  g  h  t  e  s  s  h
l  v  i  e  o  v  u  e  i
p  r  e  t  t  y  t  b  n
s  r  g  m  s  h  h  s  k
a  p  o  s  o  m  a  t  e
d  r  u  m  m  i  n  g  s
d  e  u  e  e  n  k  e  b
t  l  e  a  p  e  t  a  l
```

C Fill in the boxes with the correct spelling words.

1. 2. 3.

DAY
3

Words with *th-*

these	think	pretty
those	thank	eight

A **Use the correct spelling words to complete the story.**

One spring, the boys down the block saw baby ducks on their pond. They counted _____ ducks swimming near the dock.

They had to _____ about how to make friends with ducks. They took bread to feed the ducks. When the ducks saw the boys on the dock, they swam away. The boys sat still for a very long time. They waited for the ducks to come back. The boys made friends with the baby ducks by feeding them and being very still. They fed them every day after school. Now _____ eight ducklings follow the boys everywhere.

B **Write each spelling word three times.**

1. pretty _____ _____ _____

2. think _____ _____ _____

3. those _____ _____ _____

4. thank _____ _____ _____

5. these _____ _____ _____

6. eight _____ _____ _____

© 2001 Steck-Vaughn Company. All Rights Reserved.

Name _____

DAY
4

Words with *th-*

these	think	pretty
those	thank	eight

A Write each spelling word two times in cursive.

think _____

eight _____

pretty _____

those _____

these _____

thank _____

B Circle the word that is the same as the top one.

think	pretty	these	eight	those	thank
thnik	preffy	those	eihgt	these	thank
think	prettg	tkese	ieght	fhose	think
thkin	pretty	thesc	eight	thosc	thnak
thunk	pnetty	these	eigth	those	thunk

C Complete each sentence.

1. I think _____.

2. That is a pretty _____.

Review

bank	collar	hurt
ranch	pinch	these
branch	inch	class
thank	strung	drank
dollar	swung	those

A **Match each picture with its word. Then write the word.**

1. collar _____

2. ranch _____

3. branch _____

B **Fill in each blank with the correct spelling word.**

1. My art _____ went on a trip to a museum.
   _{class   collar}

2. Do you think _____ houses need new paint?
   _{these   thank}

3. _____ you for giving me a ride to the store.
   _{Think   Thank}

4. _____ bushes across the street need to be trimmed.
   _{Thank   Those}

5. Does your head _____ ?
   _{bank   hurt}

© 2001 Steck-Vaughn Company. All Rights Reserved.

Name _____

after	trust	junk
today	trip	wink
eight	pretty	think
club	blink	full
together	trunk	again

C **Find the missing letters. Then write the word.**

1. p r _____ _____ _____ y   _____

2. a _____ _____ _____ n   _____

3. _____ _____ _____ s t   _____

4. j _____ _____ _____   _____

5. b l _____ _____ _____   _____

6. t _____ in _____   _____

D **Use the correct spelling words to complete the story.**

Last night we did not sleep a _____. We were

excited because our travel club is going on a _____ to

Spain.

We leave for our trip _____. We will pack our

_____ backpacks in the _____ of our car.

Hopefully the trunk will not be too _____. On the way

to the airport, we will stop at the bank to pick up our traveler's

checks. We can't wait to take this trip!

Words with *-et* and *-it*

DAY 1

basket	rabbit	about
blanket	visit	hive

A Circle the spelling word. Then write it on the line.

1. Tell me about your grandmother. _____

2. I threw the ball into the basket. _____

3. Bees fly into their hive. _____

4. The animal with big ears was a rabbit. _____

5. I have a warm blanket for my bed. _____

6. I would like to visit my uncle. _____

B Fill in each blank with a spelling word.

1. Have you ever been to _____ that museum?

2. We have a pet _____.

3. What is that story _____?

4. Please put your dirty clothes in the laundry _____.

5. The _____ is full of bees.

6. I put a _____ on my bed when it was cold last week.

C Write a word that ends like each spelling word below.

bask<u>et</u>   hiv<u>e</u>   rabb<u>it</u>   ab<u>out</u>

_____   _____   _____   _____

© 2001 Steck-Vaughn Company. All Rights Reserved.

Name _____

Words with *-et* and *-it*

basket	rabbit	about
blanket	visit	hive

DAY 2

A Use the correct spelling words to complete the story.

What a fine day for a picnic! Let's fill a _____ with good things to eat. I'll pack apples, cheese, fresh bread, and grapes. We'll _____ our favorite spot in the woods by the stream. It is such a pretty place.

I'll spread a _____ under an oak tree. Then we'll eat our food. After that, we can skip rocks in the stream. And when we get tired, we'll rest in the shade and talk _____ the fun we had.

B Fill in the boxes with the correct spelling words.

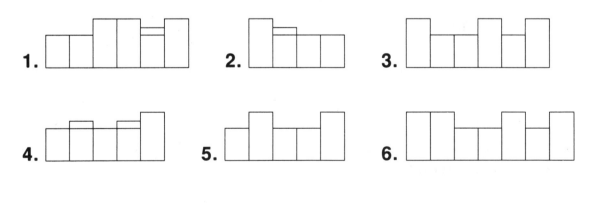

1.

2.

3.

4.

5.

6.

C Put an *X* on the word that is <u>not</u> the same.

1. blanket   blanket   blanhet   blanket   blanket

2. about   about   about   about   aboat

Words with *-et* and *-it*

basket	rabbit	about
blanket	visit	hive

DAY 3

A Write the spelling words in ABC order.

1. _____ 2. _____ 3. _____

4. _____ 5. _____ 6. _____

B Write words that begin like each spelling word below.

<u>h</u>ive   <u>b</u>asket   <u>v</u>isit   <u>bl</u>anket

_____   _____   _____   _____

_____   _____   _____   _____

_____   _____   _____   _____

C Complete each sentence.

1. I will <u>visit</u> _____.

2. My pet <u>rabbit</u> _____.

3. The <u>basket</u> was full of _____.

D Find the missing letters. Then write the word.

1. b _____ _____ _____ e t   _____

2. a b _____ _____ _____   _____

3. v i s _____ _____   _____

© 2001 Steck-Vaughn Company. All Rights Reserved.

Name _____

71

Words with -*et* and -*it*

basket	rabbit	about
blanket	visit	hive

A Circle the word that is the same as the top one.

about	rabbit	basket	blanket	visit	hive
aboat	rabdit	bisket	blanket	wisit	hvie
aboot	ribbet	basket	blonket	visit	hiev
about	rabbit	boshet	blinket	visif	hive
abuot	rabbif	bashet	blunket	visik	have

B Write each spelling word two times in cursive.

hive

basket

about

rabbit

visit

blanket

C Answer each question with a spelling word.

1. Which word begins with two consonants? _____

2. Which word contains three vowels? _____

Words with -or and -om

doctor	bottom	use
visitor	seldom	saw

DAY 1

A **Circle the spelling word. Then write it on the line.**

1. You can see the bottom of the lake. _____

2. Do you know how to use that tool? _____

3. My friend was a visitor at the art show. _____

4. I live so far away that I seldom see you. _____

5. When I was sick, I went to the doctor. _____

6. I saw you at the store last Friday. _____

B **Write the spelling words in ABC order.**

1. _____ 2. _____ 3. _____

4. _____ 5. _____ 6. _____

C **Fill in each blank with a spelling word.**

1. My power _____ cuts wood.

2. The _____ of my lunch bag fell out.

3. How many times have you been to the _____ this year?

4. A _____ came to our office.

5. We _____ miss our favorite TV show.

© 2001 Steck-Vaughn Company. All Rights Reserved.

Name _____

Words with *-or* and *-om*

doctor	bottom	use
visitor	seldom	saw

A Use the correct spelling words to complete the story.

My sister wanted to make a table. She bought some wood and nails. Since she _____ used a saw, she didn't have one of her own. So she used her friend's. But her friend's _____ was rusty. It had to be cleaned before it was ready to _____. My sister made a nice table. It's still in our kitchen. We eat at it each day.

B Circle the word that is the same as the top one.

doctor	visitor	bottom	seldom	use	saw
boctor	visitor	botton	saldom	vse	was
docfor	visiter	dottom	seldom	usc	sav
docton	viseter	buttom	suldom	use	sow
doctor	visater	bottom	soldom	nse	saw

C Complete each sentence.

1. We <u>seldom</u> go _____.

2. I know how to <u>use</u> _____.

74

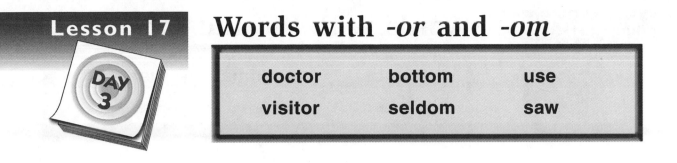

Words with *-or* **and** *-om*

DAY 3

doctor	bottom	use
visitor	seldom	saw

A Write each spelling word two times in cursive.

seldom _____

doctor _____

visitor _____

use _____

bottom _____

saw _____

B Write words that end like each spelling word below.

doct<u>or</u>   botto<u>m</u>   sa<u>w</u>   us<u>e</u>

_____   _____   _____   _____

_____   _____   _____   _____

C Fill in the boxes with the correct spelling words.

1. ▢▢▢▢▢▢▢   2. ▢▢▢   3. ▢▢▢▢▢▢

D Complete the sentence.

I took the <u>visitor</u> _____ .

Name _____

© 2001 Steck-Vaughn Company. All Rights Reserved.

Words with *-or* and *-om*

doctor	bottom	use
visitor	seldom	saw

A Find the hidden spelling words.

```
p  e  o  p  l  e  t  t  s  h  b
u  a  v  o  o  a  e  e  p  u  o
s  e  l  d  o  m  l  a  u  g  t
e  e  n  r  e  r  l  o  d  a  t
o  v  i  s  i  t  o  r  i  d  o
m  e  f  b  i  a  f  g  n  r  m
e  r  d  o  c  t  o  r  s  o  e
o  y  u  t  e  a  v  s  a  w  r
```

B Write each spelling word three times.

1. seldom _____ _____ _____

2. use _____ _____ _____

3. doctor _____ _____ _____

4. saw _____ _____ _____

5. visitor _____ _____ _____

6. bottom _____ _____ _____

C Find the missing letters. Then write the word.

d _____ _____ _____ _____ _____   _____

Lesson 18 — Words with *-ic* and *-ty*

DAY 1

traffic	empty	say
picnic	fifty	their

A Circle the spelling word. Then write it on the line.

1. It's a pretty day for a picnic. _____

2. The milk carton is empty. _____

3. The team won their game today. _____

4. The traffic is bad downtown. _____

5. Two quarters are the same as fifty cents. _____

6. I'd like to say a few words. _____

B Fill in the boxes with the correct spelling words.

1.

2.

3.

C Fill in each blank with a spelling word.

1. Your stomach feels _____ when you are hungry.

2. How much did you _____ this cup cost?

3. At five o'clock the _____ is bad.

4. They bought _____ new car today.

5. Let's have a _____ lunch in the park this afternoon.

Name _____

© 2001 Steck-Vaughn Company. All Rights Reserved.

Words with *-ic* and *-ty*

traffic	empty	say
picnic	fifty	their

A Write the spelling words in ABC order.

1. _____ 2. _____ 3. _____

4. _____ 5. _____ 6. _____

B Circle the word that is the same as the top one.

traffic	picnic	empty	fifty	their	say
lraffic	pacnic	empty	fefty	thier	saq
tnaffic	picnic	enpty	fofty	their	saw
traffic	picnoc	emqty	forty	thein	sav
treffic	pienic	emdty	fifty	fheir	say

C Find the missing letters. Then write the word.

1. t r ____ ____ f ____ ____   _____

2. p ____ ____ n ____ ____   _____

3. ____ m ____ ____ ____   _____

D Use spelling words in two sentences.

1. _____

2. _____

DAY 3

Words with *-ic* and *-ty*

traffic	empty	say
picnic	fifty	their

A **Use the correct spelling words to complete the story.**

Our friends had a party in the park. _____ people came. We all brought _____ lunches. We played a game of baseball. Then it was time to eat.

"Hey, my lunch sack is _____!" cried a girl. I looked in my sack. It was empty, too. Then we saw a trail of food leading to the woods. "Let's see what took our food," she said.

"What if it's a bear?" I asked. We decided not to check the woods. Other people shared _____ food with us. We never knew what took our food.

B **Write each spelling word three times.**

1. picnic _____ _____ _____

2. empty _____ _____ _____

3. their _____ _____ _____

C **Write these spelling words from other lessons.**

1. those _____   2. swimming _____

3. blanket _____   4. visit _____

5. doctor _____   6. seldom _____

© 2001 Steck-Vaughn Company. All Rights Reserved.

Name _____

79

Words with *-ic* and *-ty*

DAY 4

traffic	empty	say
picnic	fifty	their

A Write each spelling word two times in cursive.

fifty

picnic

traffic

empty

say

their

B Put an **X** on the word that is **not** the same.

1. fifty	fifty	fifty	fitfy	fifty
2. picnic	picnic	qicnic	picnic	picnic
3. their	their	their	their	thier
4. say	say	soy	say	say
5. traffic	traffic	traffic	tnaffic	traffic

C Fill in the boxes with the correct spelling words.

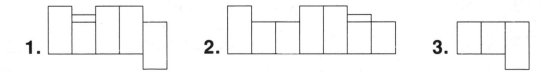

1.   2.   3.

Words with -*le* and -*al*

bottle	signal	been
candle	petal	before

DAY 1

A **Circle the spelling word. Then write it on the line.**

1. You should signal before you turn. _____

2. The petal fell off the flower. _____

3. The vanilla candle smells good. _____

4. Just before lunch, it began to rain. _____

5. I have been sick since yesterday. _____

6. The baby drinks from a bottle. _____

B **Fill in each blank with a spelling word.**

1. The bee landed on a rose _____.

2. Run for home plate when I give the _____.

3. Spring comes _____ summer.

4. Have you _____ doing all your work?

5. Which _____ of soda is yours?

6. If the lights go out, use a _____.

C **Write the spelling words in ABC order.**

1. _____   2. _____   3. _____

4. _____   5. _____   6. _____

Name _____

© 2001 Steck-Vaughn Company. All Rights Reserved.

Words with -*le* and -*al*

bottle	signal	been
candle	petal	before

A Circle the word that is the same as the top one.

bottle	been	candle	before	signal	petal
battle	bean	candle	betore	sigral	betal
bittle	beeu	caudle	before	signal	batel
bottle	deen	cardle	befone	sigual	petal
bottel	been	cnadle	befoue	sigmal	detal

B Use the correct spelling words to complete the story.

It was dark outside and raining hard. I was trying to read a book. But the lights had _____ going on and off during the storm. So I found a _____. Then I found a match in the kitchen and lit the candle.

_____ long, the lights went out and didn't come back on for the rest of the night. I was glad I had found the candle. I finished my book by the candle's light.

C Find the missing letters. Then write the word.

1. s _____ _____ n _____ l   _____

2. b e _____ _____ _____ e   _____

Lesson 19

 DAY 3

Words with *-le* and *-al*

| bottle | signal | been |
| candle | petal | before |

A **Find the hidden spelling words.**

```
b  t  l  e  a  p  e  t  a  l  s
e  e  u  a  d  b  a  o  n  e  i
f  a  n  t  d  o  t  s  y  s  g
o  c  c  y  e  t  i  s  o  s  n
r  h  h  o  d  t  n  o  n  o  a
e  r  b  s  o  l  b  e  e  n  l
d  i  e  u  i  e  e  n  v  s  p
a  g  a  c  a  n  d  l  e  o  e
y  n  s  e  d  i  o  t  r  u  n
```

B **Write each spelling word three times.**

1. candle _____ _____ _____

2. been _____ _____ _____

3. petal _____ _____ _____

4. bottle _____ _____ _____

5. before _____ _____ _____

6. signal _____ _____ _____

C **Complete the sentence.**

Before Saturday, _____.

Name _____

 © 2001 Steck-Vaughn Company. All Rights Reserved.

83

Words with -*le* and -*al*

bottle	signal	been
candle	petal	before

A Write each spelling word two times in cursive.

bottle _____

been _____

signal _____

candle _____

petal _____

before _____

B Put an *X* on the word that is <u>not</u> the same.

1. bottle	bottle	bottle	battle	bottle
2. been	been	beef	been	been
3. signal	signal	signal	signal	siqnal
4. candle	caudle	candle	candle	candle
5. petal	petal	pefal	petal	petal

C Fill in the boxes with the correct spelling words.

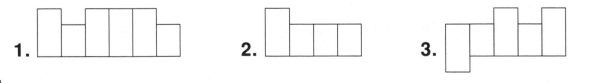

1. _____ 2. _____ 3. _____

Words with *-on* and *-ly*

DAY 1

melon	happily	mind
lemon	sadly	there

A Circle the spelling word. Then write it on the line.

1. A cantaloupe is a melon. _____

2. There is that sock I lost! _____

3. Do you mind if we watch this show? _____

4. A lemon can taste very sour. _____

5. The baby played happily in his crib. _____

6. We sadly said goodbye to them. _____

B Fill in each blank with a spelling word.

1. I like to eat ripe, sweet _____.

2. Do you _____ if I sit next to you?

3. I will _____ help you wash the dishes.

4. The honey is over _____ on the table.

5. Do you like _____ in your iced tea?

6. She cried _____ when she lost her cat.

C Write the spelling words in ABC order.

1. _____   2. _____   3. _____

4. _____   5. _____   6. _____

© 2001 Steck-Vaughn Company. All Rights Reserved.

Name _____

DAY 2

Words with -*on* and -*ly*

melon	happily	mind
lemon	sadly	there

A Circle the word that is the same as the top one.

lemon	there	sadly	melon	mind	happily
lewon	tnere	sably	nelon	wind	happily
lemou	there	sadlv	meton	minb	hoppily
lemon	thore	sodly	melou	mind	heppily
lcmon	thare	sadly	melon	miud	happely

B Use the correct spelling words to complete the story.

My friend called early this morning. "Come see my new car," he said. I ran _____ down the street to his house. He led me into the garage. "_____ it is," he said.

It was the best-looking car I'd ever seen. I wanted one just like it. "Would you _____ if I took it for a drive?" I asked my friend. I was glad that he didn't mind at all.

C Find the missing letters. Then write the word.

1. _____ _____ e r e   _____

2. m _____ _____ _____   _____

Words with *-on* and *-ly*

melon	happily	mind
lemon	sadly	there

 A Find the hidden spelling words.

```
b  n  s  t  f  b  y  e  m  h
h  e  l  f  h  a  m  g  a  s
a  t  h  e  r  e  o  a  f  a
p  h  o  o  t  l  a  p  a  d
p  m  i  n  d  e  a  t  l  l
i  s  p  r  o  m  p  t  l  y
l  s  p  a  c  o  r  u  e  o
y  m  e  l  o  n  a  r  t  u
a  i  a  a  f  o  y  k  u  t
```

B Write each spelling word three times.

1. happily _____ _____ _____

2. lemon _____ _____ _____

3. mind _____ _____ _____

4. melon _____ _____ _____

5. sadly _____ _____ _____

6. there _____ _____ _____

C Complete the sentence.

This <u>lemon</u> is _____.

Name _____

© 2001 Steck-Vaughn Company. All Rights Reserved.

Words with -*on* and -*ly*

DAY
4

melon	happily	mind
lemon	sadly	there

 A Write each spelling word two times in cursive.

mind _____

melon _____

lemon _____

there _____

sadly _____

happily _____

B Fill in the boxes with the correct spelling words.

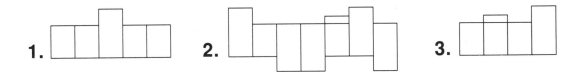

1.   2.   3.

C Put an *X* on the word that is <u>not</u> the same.

1.	sadly	sadly	sably	sadly	sadly
2.	mind	mind	mind	mind	minb
3.	there	thene	there	there	there
4.	happily	happily	happily	hoppily	happily

about	been	blanket
picnic	seldom	basket
candle	lemon	rabbit
use	empty	visit
petal	fifty	saw

A **Match each picture with its word. Then write the word.**

1. lemon _____

2. rabbit _____

3. candle _____

B **Fill in each blank with a spelling word.**

1. We learned _____ tornadoes in our science class.

2. I _____ miss my favorite show.

3. The carton of milk was _____.

4. How many of you _____ the full moon last night?

5. Have you ever _____ to the beach?

Name _____

© 2001 Steck-Vaughn Company. All Rights Reserved.

Review

before	hive	signal
bottle	melon	traffic
bottom	mind	their
doctor	sadly	there
visitor	happily	say

C Find the missing letters. Then write the word.

1. _____ _____ _____ l y   _____

2. b _____ _____ _____ _____ m   _____

3. v _____ s _____ _____ _____ r   _____

4. m _____ _____ _____ _____   _____

5. _____ _____ _____ _____ f i c   _____

6. s _____ _____   _____

7. _____ _____ _____ i r   _____

D Use the correct spelling words to complete the story.

Last week I learned a hard lesson. I saw several bees flying

around a _____. I think I got a little too close because

the bees stung me on my legs and arms. I began to swell, so

my friend drove me to see a _____ at the hospital. We

had a hard time getting _____ because the traffic was

bad. But my friend turned on his car's emergency _____

so we could get through the traffic. We made it there in no time!

Words with *st-* and *sk-*

studies	skate	carry
studied	skin	off

A Circle the spelling word. Then write it on the line.

1. My friend studies all the time. _____

2. I studied for my math test. _____

3. Do you like to skate? _____

4. I can't carry all these books. _____

5. Skin covers your bones. _____

6. Turn the lights off when you leave. _____

B Fill in each blank with a spelling word.

1. Have you _____ your spelling words?

2. We scraped the ice _____ the windows.

3. Be careful not to sunburn your _____.

4. Can you help me _____ my books to class?

5. Do you like to _____ on ice?

6. I hope everyone _____ spelling each day.

C Fill in the boxes with the correct spelling words.

1. ☐☐☐   2. ☐☐☐   3. ☐☐☐☐☐

© 2001 Steck-Vaughn Company. All Rights Reserved.

Name _____

DAY
2

Words with *st-* and *sk-*

studies	skate	carry
studied	skin	off

A Write the spelling words in ABC order.

1. _____ 2. _____ 3. _____

4. _____ 5. _____ 6. _____

B Use the correct spelling words to complete the story.

Winter is my favorite time of year. The lake freezes over,

and we go there to _____ on the ice. I like to go in

the afternoon, when all my _____ are done.

We can even skate after dark. There are lights on the

shore of the lake. The lights go _____ at eight. But

by then, everyone is ready to go home and drink hot tea or

hot chocolate.

C Circle the word that is the same as the top one.

skate	off	carry	studies	skin	studied
shate	oft	carvy	studies	shin	studies
skate	otf	carny	studied	skin	stubied
skaet	off	carrg	studics	skim	sfudied
skeat	ott	carry	sfudies	sken	studied

Words with *st-* and *sk-*

DAY 3

studies	skate	carry
studied	skin	off

A Find the hidden spelling words.

```
g  r  a  s  s  e  s  e  a  t  e  d  c
b  a  g  b  o  a  t  h  i  s  s  b  r
s  k  a  t  e  a  u  a  n  e  o  o  a
a  s  o  a  f  b  d  m  k  n  m  f  t
s  l  s  t  u  d  i  e  s  t  e  f  e
p  a  e  o  r  f  e  m  p  t  i  e  s
e  m  p  t  i  e  d  a  s  k  i  n  e
a  e  a  e  c  a  i  n  n  e  o  d  n
r  n  n  c  a  r  r  y  s  y  f  s  d
```

B Write these spelling words from other lessons.

1. signal _____

2. empty _____

3. plenty _____

4. lemon _____

C Write each spelling word three times.

1. carry _____ _____ _____

2. studies _____ _____ _____

3. off _____ _____ _____

4. studied _____ _____ _____

Name _____

© 2001 Steck-Vaughn Company. All Rights Reserved.

DAY
4

Words with *st-* and *sk-*

studies	skate	carry
studied	skin	off

 A   Write each spelling word two times in cursive.

skin

skate

carry

off

studies

studied

 B   Use spelling words in two sentences.

1. _____

2. _____

C   Put an *X* on the word that is <u>not</u> the same.

1. off	off	off	oft	off
2. studies	studies	stubies	studies	studies
3. carry	carny	carry	carry	carry
4. skin	skin	skin	skin	shin
5. skate	skate	skate	skute	skate

Words with -ful

cupful	helpful	too
handful	seven	under

DAY 1

A **Circle the spelling word. Then write it on the line.**

1. I am too sick to go to work today. _____

2. She has a handful of marbles. _____

3. The recipe calls for a cupful of sugar. _____

4. I have seven sisters and brothers. _____

5. Are you helpful around the house? _____

6. The dog likes to sleep under the steps. _____

B **Fill in each blank with a spelling word.**

1. My brother is _____ years old.

2. My sister is very _____ in the yard.

3. The box was _____ big to fit through the door.

4. We ran _____ the umbrella when the rain began.

5. Put a _____ of dirt over the seeds.

6. To make this cake, I need a _____ of flour.

C **Write the spelling words in ABC order.**

1. _____ 2. _____ 3. _____

4. _____ 5. _____ 6. _____

Name _____

© 2001 Steck-Vaughn Company. All Rights Reserved.

Words with -*ful*

cupful	helpful	too
handful	seven	under

A Use the correct spelling words to complete the story.

The prince was unhappy being just a prince. "I want to be a great cook," he said. So he went to the palace cook for lessons. The cook told him to watch and learn.

"Use a _____ of this and a _____ of that," she told him. Cooking looked _____ hard for the prince. He decided to find something easier to do.

B Circle the word that is the same as the top one.

under	too	seven	handful	helpful	cupful
udner	foo	sever	bandful	helpful	oupful
umder	too	seven	nandful	helbful	copful
unber	toa	svene	handful	helbfnl	cubful
under	taa	sewer	dandful	helpfnl	cupful

C Find the missing letters. Then write the word.

1. c u ____ ____ ____ l   _____

2. ____ ____ n d ____ ____ ____   _____

3. h e ____ ____ f ____ ____   _____

Words with *-ful*

cupful	helpful	too
handful	seven	under

A Find the hidden spelling words.

```
y  n  s  e  d  i  o  t  r  u  n
t  t  o  a  s  t  r  i  p  s  p
r  o  s  e  v  e  n  o  p  o  e
o  m  o  p  o  e  c  a  e  m  o
o  o  m  p  n  n  e  d  c  e  p
t  r  e  h  e  l  p  f  u  l  l
o  r  s  e  e  i  u  o  p  h  e
o  o  o  a  s  l  f  u  f  i  p
l  w  u  n  d  e  r  a  u  n  a
s  i  h  a  n  d  f  u  l  g  p
o  n  o  f  f  a  o  n  a  r  e
a  g  a  s  e  s  f  e  e  o  e
```

B Write each spelling word three times.

1. seven _____ _____ _____

2. handful _____ _____ _____

3. helpful _____ _____ _____

4. cupful _____ _____ _____

5. too _____ _____ _____

6. under _____ _____ _____

Name _____

© 2001 Steck-Vaughn Company. All Rights Reserved.

Words with *-ful*

cupful	helpful	too
handful	seven	under

A Write each spelling word two times in cursive.

helpful

seven

handful

cupful

under

too

B Put an *X* on the word that is <u>not</u> the same.

1.	under	under	unber	under	under
2.	seven	seven	seven	seven	sever
3.	too	too	too	too	foo
4.	helpful	helptul	helpful	helpful	helpful

C Fill in the boxes with the correct spelling words.

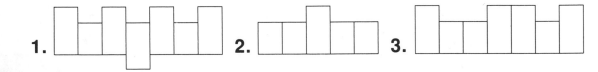

1.   2.   3.

Lesson 23

Words with *sh-*

shall	shell	want
shack	shelf	first

A **Circle the spelling word. Then write it on the line.**

1. The small cabin is a shack. _____

2. We keep the cans on the shelf. _____

3. How much salad do you want? _____

4. I was first in line at the store. _____

5. I found a shell on the beach. _____

6. How much shall I pay for this tie? _____

B **Fill in each blank with a spelling word.**

1. I found a pretty _____ at the beach.

2. Do you _____ to go to the movies?

3. We keep our tools in a _____ outside.

4. Please put the books back on the _____.

5. How often _____ I take out the trash?

6. Who came in _____ in the three-legged race?

C **Write the spelling words in ABC order.**

1. _____ 2. _____ 3. _____

4. _____ 5. _____ 6. _____

Name _____

© 2001 Steck-Vaughn Company. All Rights Reserved.

DAY 2

Words with *sh-*

shall	shell	want
shack	shelf	first

A Use the correct spelling words to complete the story.

I love to walk on the beach. You should see what I find there. Once I found a _____ that looked like an ear. There was a hole in it, so I made the shell into a necklace.

I also have three perfect sand dollars. I _____ to show off all my shells. But _____ I need to build a _____ to put them on.

B Circle the word that is the same as the top one.

<u>want</u>	<u>first</u>	<u>shack</u>	<u>shell</u>	<u>shelf</u>	<u>shall</u>
went	finst	shack	skell	shelt	shell
wont	firsf	shuck	shell	shelf	sholl
want	tirst	shock	shall	shalf	shall
what	first	snack	shcll	sholf	snall

C Put an X on the word that is <u>not</u> the same.

1. shall   shall   shell   shall   shall

2. want   wart   want   want   want

3. first   first   first   finst   first

DAY
3

Words with *sh-*

shall	shell	want
shack	shelf	first

A **Find the hidden spelling words.**

```
s  m  e  l  o  n  a  r  t  u  b  n  s
s  t  e  e  r  r  h  w  a  n  t  a  b
s  l  e  e  p  a  o  e  p  o  e  l  s
h  e  a  r  o  s  r  a  p  r  n  l  h
a  m  n  b  c  h  s  t  l  t  l  a  a
l  r  o  o  v  s  e  h  e  h  e  u  c
l  o  n  g  b  h  e  e  s  s  s  g  k
a  v  e  n  u  e  l  r  w  i  s  h  r
a  s  t  a  l  l  f  s  h  e  l  l  k
b  l  u  e  o  f  f  i  r  s  t  w  i
s  o  m  e  m  e  e  t  r  b  s  v  d
a  s  p  a  c  o  r  u  e  o  a  i  a
```

B **Write each spelling word three times.**

1. shall _____ _____ _____

2. want _____ _____ _____

3. shack _____ _____ _____

4. first _____ _____ _____

5. shell _____ _____ _____

6. shelf _____ _____ _____

Name _____

© 2001 Steck-Vaughn Company. All Rights Reserved.

DAY 4

Words with *sh-*

shall	shell	want
shack	shelf	first

A Write each spelling word two times in cursive.

shack _____

shell _____

shelf _____

shall _____

first _____

want _____

B Fill in the boxes with the correct spelling words.

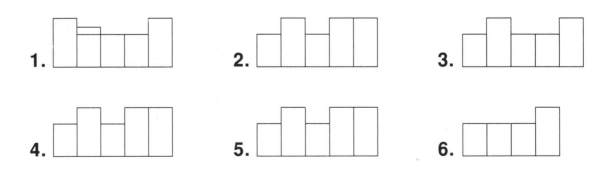

1.

2.

3.

4.

5.

6.

C Find the missing letters. Then write the word.

1. _____ _____ a c k   _____

2. _____ _____ e l f   _____

3. w a _____ _____   _____

DAY 1

Words with *sh-*

ship	shock	both
shift	shop	does

A **Circle the spelling word. Then write it on the line.**

1. Do you like to shop at the market? _____

2. Where does your mother work? _____

3. Can you drive a stick shift car? _____

4. Be careful, that wire may shock you. _____

5. That ship sails across the ocean. _____

6. Raise both arms at the same time. _____

B **Fill in each blank with a spelling word.**

1. If you touch the light switch with wet hands, you might

    get a _____.

2. Do you know how to _____ the gears in a car?

3. My mother went to _____ for a new coat.

4. This woman is the captain of the _____.

5. Look _____ ways before you cross the street.

C **Use spelling words in two sentences.**

1. _____

2. _____

Name _____

© 2001 Steck-Vaughn Company. All Rights Reserved.

DAY
2

Words with *sh-*

ship	shock	both
shift	shop	does

A Use the correct spelling words to complete the story.

My younger brother bought a new bike. Boy, was he in for

a _____. The bike had ten gears! It took him a week

to learn to _____ them all. "They didn't tell me about

this at the _____," he said.

But he soon learned to ride like a champ. He even learned

how to fix the bike if it breaks.

B Circle the word that is the same as the top one.

both	shift	does	ship	shock	shop
bath	chift	doez	ship	shack	ship
bafh	shlft	boes	shop	shuck	shop
doth	shift	deos	shap	shock	shob
both	shiff	does	skip	shoch	skop

C Complete each sentence.

1. I like to <u>shop</u> _____.

2. <u>Both</u> of the girls _____.

Words with *sh-*

ship	shock	both
shift	shop	does

DAY 3

A Find the hidden spelling words.

```
s a v s a h t y r a a o
s d a r k e w s e e m y
h f l e e a h h i l l e
i m a n y s o i l e t s
f o o i s h o p f l d g
t o f f e o i a a a o i
b d r p a c l c s m e r
l b o t h k l k t b s l
a e a e e s e e a b e b
```

B Write each spelling word three times.

1. shop _____ _____ _____

2. both _____ _____ _____

3. ship _____ _____ _____

4. does _____ _____ _____

C Write these spelling words from other lessons.

1. flute _____   **2.** studies _____

3. cupful _____   **4.** want _____

© 2001 Steck-Vaughn Company. All Rights Reserved.

Name _____

Lesson 24

DAY 4

Words with *sh-*

ship	shock	both
shift	shop	does

A Write each spelling word two times in cursive.

shock

shop

shift

ship

both

does

B Put an *X* on the word that is <u>not</u> the same.

1. both	bath	both	both	both
2. ship	ship	ship	skip	ship
3. shop	shop	shop	shop	snop
4. does	does	boes	does	does
5. shock	shock	shock	shoch	shock

C Fill in the boxes with the correct spelling words.

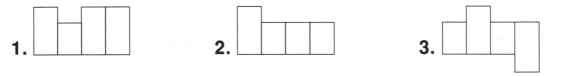

1.   **2.**   **3.**

DAY 1

Words with *wh-*

what	which	thunder
white	when	shut

A Circle the spelling word. Then write it on the line.

1. Have you ever seen a white rose? _____

2. Please shut the door. _____

3. I can hear the loud thunder. _____

4. What is your name? _____

5. I can't tell which book is mine. _____

6. When do you go to bed? _____

B Fill in each blank with a spelling word.

1. _____ house is yours?

2. Please _____ all the windows because it is going to rain.

3. The _____ woke me up in the middle of the night.

4. _____ time is it?

5. _____ will it be time to eat?

6. Snow is _____.

C Use spelling words in two sentences.

1. _____

2. _____

Name _____

© 2001 Steck-Vaughn Company. All Rights Reserved.

Words with *wh-*

what	which	thunder
white	when	shut

A Write words that begin like each spelling word below.

<u>wh</u>at   <u>sh</u>ut   <u>th</u>under

_____   _____   _____

_____   _____   _____

B Circle the word that is the same as the top one.

<u>white</u>	<u>which</u>	<u>what</u>	<u>when</u>	<u>shut</u>	<u>thunder</u>
mhite	whach	whot	whin	snut	thumber
whlitt	whuch	whaf	when	shut	thunder
white	which	mhat	whun	shnt	thunber
wnite	whoch	what	whon	shuf	thnuder

C Write the spelling word that rhymes with the word pair.

1. nut   cut   _____

2. ten   pen   _____

3. bite   kite   _____

D Find the missing letters. Then write the word.

t h ____ ____ d e r   _____

Words with *wh-*

what	which	thunder
white	when	shut

A **Use the correct spelling words to complete the story.**

My dog Olly is scared of loud noises. He's especially afraid

of _____. It makes him shake all over. He hides

under the bed _____ there's a storm. I asked the vet

_____ to do about Olly. "Pet him and talk to him in

a soft voice," she said.

But this didn't seem to help. Then I got an idea. The next

time there was a storm, I got the headphones for my radio. I

put them on Olly's ears. It worked! He didn't shake or hide

under the bed.

B **Write the spelling words in ABC order.**

1. _____   2. _____   3. _____

4. _____   5. _____   6. _____

C **Write each spelling word three times.**

1. shut   _____   _____   _____

2. white   _____   _____   _____

3. what   _____   _____   _____

4. thunder   _____   _____   _____

Name _____

© 2001 Steck-Vaughn Company. All Rights Reserved.

Words with *wh-*

what	**which**	**thunder**
white	**when**	**shut**

A Write each spelling word two times in cursive.

what

white

shut

which

when

thunder

B Put an **X** on the word that is <u>not</u> the same.

1.	when	when	when	whan	when
2.	shut	shut	shuf	shut	shut
3.	what	what	what	what	wkat
4.	white	whife	white	white	white

C Fill in the boxes with the correct spelling words.

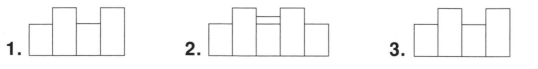

1.   2.   3.

Review

carry	shack	which
shut	shell	cupful
shelf	shock	skate
shift	first	skin
shop	want	white

A Match each picture with its word. Then write the word.

1. skate _____

2. shelf _____

3. shell _____

B Fill in each blank with a spelling word.

1. _____ room is yours?

2. Please _____ the door quickly.

3. The cook will use a _____ of flour.

4. Will you paint the door _____ or brown?

5. Do you _____ to eat at this diner tonight?

Name _____

© 2001 Steck-Vaughn Company. All Rights Reserved.

111

Review

studies	helpful	shall
studied	under	ship
when	thunder	does
what	handful	seven
both	too	off

C **Find the missing letters. Then write the word.**

1. s t ____ ____ ____ ____ s   _____

2. ____ ____ a ____ l   _____

3. d ____ ____ ____   _____

4. h e ____ p ____ ____ ____   _____

5. u n ____ ____ ____   _____

6. ____ ____ o   _____

D **Use the correct spelling words to complete the story.**

The sailors' adventure at sea last week was one they won't soon forget. The crew had just left the port _____ they found themselves in a big storm. _____ crashed around them, and lightning lit up the sky.

The captain _____ the compass carefully to keep the _____ on course. Finally the storm stopped, and the ship returned safely to port. _____ the captain and the sailors were happy to be on land!

DAY
1

Words with *ch-*

chat	check	with
champ	chest	yes

A **Circle the spelling word. Then write it on the line.**

1. Your ribs are inside your chest. _____

2. I hope you say "yes" to this question. _____

3. We had a nice chat on the telephone. _____

4. Would you like to go with me? _____

5. She is the skating champ. _____

6. Please check my paper. _____

B **Fill in each blank with a spelling word.**

1. I am the spelling _____ of my class.

2. Sit down and _____ with me for a while.

3. Will you please play tennis _____ me?

4. I paid for the dress with a _____.

5. I keep my clothes in a _____ of drawers.

6. _____, you may have some orange juice.

C **Find the missing letters. Then write the word.**

1. _____ i t h _____

2. _____ _____ a t _____

© 2001 Steck-Vaughn Company. All Rights Reserved.

Name _____

Words with ch-

chat	check	with
champ	chest	yes

A Write words that begin like each spelling word below.

<u>y</u>es   <u>ch</u>at   <u>w</u>ith

_____   _____   _____

_____   _____   _____

B Write the spelling words in ABC order.

1. _____   2. _____   3. _____

4. _____   5. _____   6. _____

C Fill in each blank with a spelling word.

1. Did you write this _____ with your own pen?

2. I'd like to have a _____ with you soon.

D Circle the word that is the same as the top one.

<u>chat</u>	<u>with</u>	<u>yes</u>	<u>champ</u>	<u>check</u>	<u>chest</u>
cnat	mith	yez	chomp	sheck	chist
chaf	with	yos	chump	check	chest
chat	wtih	yus	champ	chock	chost
cbat	whit	yes	chimp	cheek	cnest

Words with *ch-*

chat	check	with
champ	chest	yes

A   Write each spelling word two times in cursive.

with

yes

champ

chat

check

chest

B   Use spelling words in two sentences.

1. _____

2. _____

C   Fill in the boxes with the correct spelling words.

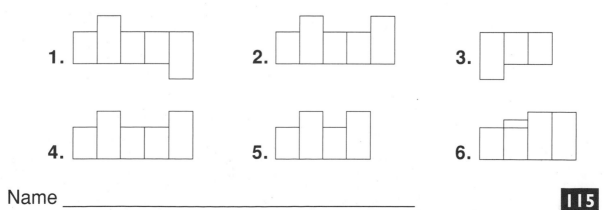

1.

2.

3.

4.

5.

6.

© 2001 Steck-Vaughn Company. All Rights Reserved.

Name _____

DAY
4

Words with *ch-*

chat	check	with
champ	chest	yes

A **Use the correct spelling words to complete the story.**

The _____ of the boxing match went to the locker

room to rest. But the fans wanted to see him. "Please

_____ with me in five minutes," the boxer told the

fans. "I need to catch my breath."

Finally, the fans went in to see the champ. They were so

proud of him. The champ was glad to visit _____ his

fans.

B **Write the spelling word that rhymes with the word pair.**

1. cat   sat   _____

2. camp   stamp   _____

3. best   rest   _____

C **Write each spelling word three times.**

1. chat   _____   _____   _____

2. champ   _____   _____   _____

3. with   _____   _____   _____

4. yes   _____   _____   _____

Lesson 27

Words with *tw-* and *qu-*

twin	quit	who
twenty	quick	will

DAY 1

A **Circle the spelling word. Then write it on the line.**

1. My sister quit taking tennis lessons. _____

2. My twin brother and I look alike. _____

3. I will not be on time for school. _____

4. Who is going to shop with you? _____

5. My friend is a very quick runner. _____

6. Twenty people came to my party. _____

B **Fill in each blank with a spelling word.**

1. _____ takes you to school?

2. Which girl is your _____ sister?

3. This is a _____ pie to make.

4. I _____ be able to go on the ski trip.

5. I cannot wait until I am _____ years old.

6. I wish you would _____ tickling me.

C **Use spelling words in two sentences.**

1. _____

2. _____

Name _____

© 2001 Steck-Vaughn Company. All Rights Reserved.

Words with *tw-* and *qu-*

DAY 2

twin	quit	who
twenty	quick	will

A Write words that begin like each spelling word below.

who   will   quit

_____   _____   _____

_____   _____   _____

B Write the spelling words in ABC order.

1. _____   2. _____   3. _____

4. _____   5. _____   6. _____

C Circle the word that is the same as the top one.

quick	who	twin	twenty	quit	will
quiet	how	tmin	twenty	puit	mill
quict	who	twim	twinty	quit	wall
guick	mho	twen	twemty	gnit	will
quick	wno	twin	twumty	gnit	wilt

D Find the missing letters. Then write the word.

1. w h _____   _____

2. t w _____ _____ t _____   _____

Words with *tw-* and *qu-*

twin	quit	who
twenty	quick	will

 A Write each spelling word two times in cursive.

who _____

will _____

twin _____

twenty _____

quit _____

quick _____

B Use the correct spelling words to complete the story.

The twins liked to play tricks on people. They looked exactly

alike. They always wore the same kind of clothes. Only their

parents could tell _____ was who. At school they

would change places and fool their teachers and friends.

"_____ teasing us," their friends would demand.

"Now, _____ you please tell us which one is which?"

Each twin would use the other twin's name. Pretty soon,

even they were mixed up. "Are you me, or am I you?" they

would ask each other and then laugh.

© 2001 Steck-Vaughn Company. All Rights Reserved.

Name _____

Words with *tw-* and *qu-*

twin	quit	who
twenty	quick	will

A Find the hidden spelling words.

```
s  n  e  d  e  d  s  o  p  s
n  m  i  n  d  e  a  t  l  l
o  w  w  e  e  q  u  i  c  k
t  h  i  p  t  u  m  c  o  e
w  o  l  o  e  i  b  i  d  y
i  e  l  l  m  t  r  n  r  s
n  e  e  d  s  h  e  g  i  o
u  v  a  r  o  o  l  c  n  m
m  e  c  e  m  u  l  a  k  e
t  w  e  n  t  y  a  k  k  o
e  y  o  m  o  a  r  e  e  n
r  i  n  e  n  n  t  s  e  e
```

B Write each spelling word three times.

1. will _____ _____ _____

2. who _____ _____ _____

3. quit _____ _____ _____

4. twenty _____ _____ _____

5. quick _____ _____ _____

6. twin _____ _____ _____

Lesson 28

Words with -ch, -sh, and -ng

bunch	flash	hang
lunch	cash	sang

A **Circle the spelling word. Then write it on the line.**

1. I saw a flash of lightning. _____

2. This is a bunch of grapes. _____

3. We eat lunch at noon. _____

4. They paid cash for the dresses. _____

5. We sang him a song on his birthday. _____

6. Please hang up your clothes. _____

B **Fill in each blank with a spelling word.**

1. Let's eat a pizza for _____.

2. I gave you ten dollars in _____.

3. A shooting star gives off a _____ of light.

4. A _____ of my friends went swimming.

5. The boy likes to _____ upside down from the tree.

6. The girls _____ a funny song.

C **Write the spelling words in ABC order.**

1. _____ 2. _____ 3. _____

4. _____ 5. _____ 6. _____

Name _____

© 2001 Steck-Vaughn Company. All Rights Reserved.

Words with *-ch, -sh,* and *-ng*

bunch	flash	hang
lunch	cash	sang

A Circle the word that is the same as the top one.

lunch	cash	bunch	hang	sang	flash
lunck	cask	bunch	hnag	snag	flash
lunkc	eash	bunhc	hang	sung	flasb
lunhc	cash	bunkc	hung	sang	flasr
lunch	casn	bunck	hong	sing	tlash

B Write words that begin like each spelling word below.

cash   bunch   flash   hang

_____   _____   _____   _____

_____   _____   _____   _____

C Fill in the boxes with the correct spelling words.

1.   2.   3.

D Find the missing letters. Then write the word.

1. h _____ _____ _____   _____

2. b _____ n _____ _____   _____

Words with *-ch, -sh,* and *-ng*

DAY 3

bunch	flash	hang
lunch	cash	sang

A Write each spelling word two times in cursive.

hang

lunch

bunch

cash

flash

sang

B Use spelling words in two sentences.

1. _____

2. _____

C Put an *X* on the word that is <u>not</u> the same.

1. cash	cash	cash	cask	cash
2. lunch	lunch	lunck	lunch	lunch
3. bunch	bunck	bunch	bunch	bunch
4. hang	hang	hang	hank	hang
5. flash	flasn	flash	flash	flash

© 2001 Steck-Vaughn Company. All Rights Reserved.

Name _____

DAY 4

Words with -*ch*, -*sh*, and -*ng*

bunch	flash	hang
lunch	cash	sang

A **Use the correct spelling words to complete the story.**

One Saturday I invited my friends over for _____.

When I looked in the kitchen, I saw we needed some things

to eat. So I went to the store to buy food. We needed bread,

chips, fruit, and drinks. When it was time to pay, I took out my

wallet. But there wasn't any _____ in my wallet.

"Please hold this food for me," I said to the man at the

store. "I'll run home for some money and be back in a

_____."

B **Write the spelling words that rhyme with the word pair.**

1. munch   crunch   _____   _____

2. dash   rash   _____   _____

3. bang   rang   _____   _____

C **Write each spelling word three times.**

1. lunch   _____   _____   _____

2. hang   _____   _____   _____

3. bunch   _____   _____   _____

4. flash   _____   _____   _____

Words with -sh

fresh	wish	because
flesh	dish	always

A **Circle the spelling word. Then write it on the line.**

1. I love fresh strawberries. _____

2. She is always happy. _____

3. He is sad because his hamster is sick. _____

4. I wish it were summer. _____

5. Please buy the cat a food dish. _____

6. Animal flesh is also called meat. _____

B **Fill in each blank with a spelling word.**

1. Before you blow out candles on a birthday cake, you

   make a _____.

2. The skinny animal did not have much _____.

3. We are having _____ green beans for dinner.

4. You are _____ fun to be around.

5. I like you _____ you are nice.

6. I dropped a _____ on the floor and broke it.

C **Complete the sentence.**

I <u>wish</u> _____.

Name _____

© 2001 Steck-Vaughn Company. All Rights Reserved.

Words with -sh

fresh	wish	because
flesh	dish	always

DAY 2

A Circle the word that is the same as the top one.

fresh	because	wish	always	flesh	dish
flesh	becavse	wash	alvays	flesh	dash
frehs	because	wish	alwavs	flash	disk
fresh	becanse	with	almays	tlesh	dish
fnesh	decause	wihs	always	flush	dizh

B Use the correct spelling words to complete the story.

One night I said to my friend, "Let's have _____ fish

for supper. We can catch the fish in the lake. Then we can

cook it on the grill."

We fished for a long time. My friend said, "I _____

we would catch a catfish. Catfish is _____ good to eat."

I said, "Wait a little longer. We'll catch a fish soon!" At dark,

we still hadn't caught a fish. We decided to try another day.

C Find the missing letters. Then write the word.

1. w _____ _____ _____   _____

2. _____ r _____ s h   _____

Words with -sh

fresh	wish	because
flesh	dish	always

A Write each spelling word two times in cursive.

fresh

flesh

because

wish

dish

always

B Fill in the boxes with the correct spelling words.

1.    2.   3.

C Put an *X* on the word that is <u>not</u> the same.

1.	dish	dish	dish	dish	disk
2.	because	because	becuase	because	because
3.	fresh	fresh	fnesh	fresh	fresh
4.	always	always	always	almays	always
5.	flesh	flesh	flcsh	flesh	flesh

© 2001 Steck-Vaughn Company. All Rights Reserved.

Name _____

DAY 4

Words with -sh

| fresh | wish | because |
| flesh | dish | always |

 A **Find the hidden spelling words.**

b s h o w i n d o w

e h i s a a m s o i

c h f g l n e e n s

a a a l w f l e s h

u m l a a d o t s a

s p l a y i v a a n

e o f e s s e l n y

i f r e s h r w d e

t o i a o o o a r s

B **Write each spelling word three times.**

1. dish _____ _____ _____

2. because _____ _____ _____

3. fresh _____ _____ _____

4. always _____ _____ _____

5. wish _____ _____ _____

6. flesh _____ _____ _____

C **Complete the sentence.**

I <u>always</u> _____.

DAY
1

Words with -*sh*

crush	rush	were
brush	hush	table

A **Circle the spelling word. Then write it on the line.**

1. I forgot to brush my hair. _____

2. We had to rush home after dinner. _____

3. Please put the books on the table. _____

4. If you say "hush", it will get quiet. _____

5. Our blender can crush ice. _____

6. They were at home when it snowed. _____

B **Fill in each blank with a spelling word.**

1. I'm in a big hurry, so I need to _____ home.

2. My sister told me to _____ because she was trying to do her homework.

3. We _____ late getting to the movie.

4. When I _____ ice, it makes a loud noise.

5. Would you like to sit at the _____?

6. Don't forget to _____ your teeth.

C **Write the spelling words in ABC order.**

1. _____   2. _____   3. _____

4. _____   5. _____   6. _____

© 2001 Steck-Vaughn Company. All Rights Reserved.

Name _____

Words with -*sh*

crush	rush	were
brush	hush	table

A Circle the word that is the same as the top one.

crush	were	brush	hush	rush	table
crash	wene	drush	hash	rush	tadle
cnash	werc	brush	hnsh	rusn	tablc
cnush	were	drnsh	shuh	rash	fable
crush	mere	brash	hush	rusk	table

B Use the correct spelling words to complete the story.

You should have seen all of us before our trip. We

_____ all running late. Our plane was to leave at

nine in the morning. We were in such a _____ that

we just left our breakfast dishes in the sink.

On the way out the front door, my sister said, "I need to

_____ my teeth!" At last we jumped in the car and

sped to the airport. We got on the plane just in time.

C Fill in the boxes with the correct spelling words.

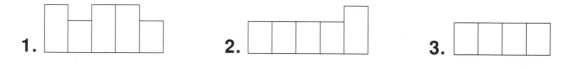

1. 2. 3.

DAY 3

Words with -*sh*

crush	rush	were
brush	hush	table

A Write each spelling word two times in cursive.

brush _____

rush _____

hush _____

table _____

were _____

crush _____

B Write these spelling words from other lessons.

1. check _____   2. because _____

3. which _____   4. wish _____

5. quick _____   6. flesh _____

C Use spelling words in four sentences.

1. _____

2. _____

3. _____

4. _____

© 2001 Steck-Vaughn Company. All Rights Reserved.

Name _____

Words with -*sh*

DAY
4

crush	rush	were
brush	hush	table

A Find the hidden spelling words.

q a s n g a s k e
c b a c k d s y h
v r r r e r e e u
a o e u e e e s s
t w a s p s b t h
w n n h i l r a l
e b i e n e u b i
r l m a g s s l t
e u a r u s h e t
b e l i r e a a l

B Write words that end like each spelling word below.

brush   table   were

_____   _____   _____

_____   _____   _____

C Write each spelling word three times.

1. were   _____   _____   _____

2. rush   _____   _____   _____

3. crush   _____   _____   _____

Review

always	chat	dish
fresh	rush	brush
check	flash	hang
sang	cash	crush
flesh	wish	table

A Match each picture with its word. Then write the word.

1.    dish   _____

2.    table   _____

3.    brush   _____

B Fill in each blank with a spelling word.

1. My friend and I had a nice _____.

2. The _____ flowers smelled good.

3. I _____ that it would snow.

4. Don't _____ the flowers when you hold them.

5. She is in a _____ to get ready for dinner.

Name _____

© 2001 Steck-Vaughn Company. All Rights Reserved.

twenty	chest	yes
twin	champ	with
lunch	hush	were
bunch	will	quick
because	who	quit

C Find the missing letters. Then write the word.

1. _____ _____ a m _____   _____

2. _____ _____ o   _____

3. _____ _____ th   _____

4. w _____ _____ l   _____

5. y _____ _____   _____

6. b _____ n _____ _____   _____

D Use the correct spelling words to complete the story.

Mr. and Mrs. Jones could hardly wait to go on their fishing

trip. Their _____ boys were so excited _____

they loved to fish. They could not wait to start fishing.

As soon as the twins put their lines in the water, the fish

began to bite. After they reeled in more than _____

fish, the twins were too tired to keep fishing. So they sat at a

picnic table and ate their _____ .

My Word List

Words I Can Spell

Put a ✓ in the box beside each word you spell correctly on your weekly test.

1

- ☐ bled
- ☐ block
- ☐ black
- ☐ blend
- ☐ woman
- ☐ wonder

2

- ☐ glad
- ☐ glass
- ☐ flag
- ☐ flip
- ☐ many
- ☐ wash

3

- ☐ plant
- ☐ plus
- ☐ slept
- ☐ slid
- ☐ small
- ☐ try

4

- ☐ scalp
- ☐ scan
- ☐ scrub
- ☐ scrap
- ☐ plenty
- ☐ brown

5

- ☐ skill
- ☐ skunk
- ☐ snap
- ☐ snack
- ☐ flute
- ☐ goes

Words To Review

If you miss a word on your test, write it here. Practice it until you can spell it correctly. Then check the box beside the word.

_____

_____

_____

_____

_____

_____

_____

_____

_____

_____

_____

_____

_____

_____

_____

Name _____

© 2001 Steck-Vaughn Company. All Rights Reserved.

My Word List

Words I Can Spell

Put a ✓ in the box beside each word you spell correctly on your weekly test.

6

- ☐ spend
- ☐ spill
- ☐ study
- ☐ stamp
- ☐ never
- ☐ warm

7

- ☐ swing
- ☐ swim
- ☐ swimming
- ☐ arm
- ☐ book
- ☐ four

8

- ☐ crust
- ☐ crack
- ☐ crash
- ☐ myself
- ☐ much
- ☐ kind

9

- ☐ drum
- ☐ drink
- ☐ grass
- ☐ grab
- ☐ frog
- ☐ done

10

- ☐ prompt
- ☐ press
- ☐ string
- ☐ strap
- ☐ group
- ☐ laugh

Words To Review

If you miss a word on your test, write it here. Practice it until you can spell it correctly. Then check the box beside the word.

_____

_____

_____

_____

_____

_____

_____

_____

_____

_____

_____

_____

_____

_____

My Word List

Words I Can Spell

Put a ✓ in the box beside each word you spell correctly on your weekly test.

11

- ☐ trip
- ☐ trust
- ☐ club
- ☐ class
- ☐ again
- ☐ after

12

- ☐ drank
- ☐ bank
- ☐ trunk
- ☐ junk
- ☐ inch
- ☐ pinch

13

- ☐ branch
- ☐ ranch
- ☐ swung
- ☐ strung
- ☐ together
- ☐ today

14

- ☐ wink
- ☐ blink
- ☐ collar
- ☐ dollar
- ☐ full
- ☐ hurt

15

- ☐ these
- ☐ those
- ☐ think
- ☐ thank
- ☐ pretty
- ☐ eight

Words To Review

If you miss a word on your test, write it here. Practice it until you can spell it correctly. Then check the box beside the word.

_____

_____

_____

_____

_____

_____

_____

_____

_____

_____

_____

_____

_____

_____

_____

Name _____

© 2001 Steck-Vaughn Company. All Rights Reserved.

My Word List

Words I Can Spell

Put a ✓ in the box beside each word you spell correctly on your weekly test.

16

- ☐ basket
- ☐ blanket
- ☐ rabbit
- ☐ visit
- ☐ about
- ☐ hive

17

- ☐ doctor
- ☐ visitor
- ☐ bottom
- ☐ seldom
- ☐ use
- ☐ saw

18

- ☐ traffic
- ☐ picnic
- ☐ empty
- ☐ fifty
- ☐ say
- ☐ their

19

- ☐ bottle
- ☐ candle
- ☐ signal
- ☐ petal
- ☐ been
- ☐ before

20

- ☐ melon
- ☐ lemon
- ☐ happily
- ☐ sadly
- ☐ mind
- ☐ there

Words To Review

If you miss a word on your test, write it here. Practice it until you can spell it correctly. Then check the box beside the word.

_____

_____

_____

_____

_____

_____

_____

_____

_____

_____

_____

_____

_____

_____

138

My Word List

Words I Can Spell

Put a ✓ in the box beside each word you spell correctly on your weekly test.

21

☐ studies   ☐ skin

☐ studied   ☐ carry

☐ skate   ☐ off

22

☐ cupful   ☐ seven

☐ handful   ☐ too

☐ helpful   ☐ under

23

☐ shall   ☐ shelf

☐ shack   ☐ want

☐ shell   ☐ first

24

☐ ship   ☐ shop

☐ shift   ☐ both

☐ shock   ☐ does

25

☐ what   ☐ when

☐ white   ☐ thunder

☐ which   ☐ shut

Words To Review

If you miss a word on your test, write it here. Practice it until you can spell it correctly. Then check the box beside the word.

_____

_____

_____

_____

_____

_____

_____

_____

_____

_____

_____

_____

_____

_____

Name _____

© 2001 Steck-Vaughn Company. All Rights Reserved.

Words I Can Spell

Put a ✓ in the box beside each word you spell correctly on your weekly test.

Words To Review

If you miss a word on your test, write it here. Practice it until you can spell it correctly. Then check the box beside the word.

——— **26** ———

- ☐ chat
- ☐ champ
- ☐ check
- ☐ chest
- ☐ with
- ☐ yes

——— **27** ———

- ☐ twin
- ☐ twenty
- ☐ quit
- ☐ quick
- ☐ who
- ☐ will

——— **28** ———

- ☐ bunch
- ☐ lunch
- ☐ flash
- ☐ cash
- ☐ hang
- ☐ sang

——— **29** ———

- ☐ fresh
- ☐ flesh
- ☐ wish
- ☐ dish
- ☐ because
- ☐ always

——— **30** ———

- ☐ crush
- ☐ brush
- ☐ rush
- ☐ hush
- ☐ were
- ☐ table

Word Study Sheet

(Make a check mark after each step.)

Name _____

Words	1 Look at the Word	2 Say the Word	3 Think About Each Letter	4 Spell the Word Aloud	5 Write the Word	6 Check the Spelling	7 Repeat Steps (if needed)

© 2001 Steck-Vaughn Company. All Rights Reserved.

Graph Your Progress

(Color or shade in the boxes.)

Number of words correctly spelled:

6						
5						
4						
3						
2						
1						

Lesson 1 · Lesson 2 · Lesson 3 · Lesson 4 · Lesson 5 · Lesson 6 · Lesson 7 · Lesson 8 · Lesson 9 · Lesson 10 · Lesson 11 · Lesson 12 · Lesson 13 · Lesson 14 · Lesson 15 · Lesson 16 · Lesson 17 · Lesson 18 · Lesson 19 · Lesson 20 · Lesson 21 · Lesson 22 · Lesson 23 · Lesson 24 · Lesson 25 · Lesson 26 · Lesson 27 · Lesson 28 · Lesson 29 · Lesson 30

Name _____